THE
TAFF
TRAIL
OFFICIAL GUIDEBOOK

The generous financial support that Esso UK plc has given to the development of the Taff Trail is greatly appreciated by Merthyr & Cynon Groundwork Trust.

This book has been produced with support from the Countryside Council for Wales, for which the Merthyr & Cynon Groundwork Trust is most grateful.

A lone cyclist crosses the Monmouthshire and Brecon Canal at Talybont-on-Usk, heading south towards Torpantau and Merthyr Tydfil. Do not be deceived by the mountain bike: much of the Taff Trail is suitable for ordinary bicycles as well (Merthyr & Cynon Groundwork Trust/ Hamish Park)

THE TAFF TRAIL

OFFICIAL GUIDEBOOK

JEFF VINTER

SUTTON PUBLISHING LIMITED

MERTHYR & CYNON GROUNDWORK TRUST

First published in 1993

Alan Sutton Publishing Limited, an imprint of Sutton Publishing Limited
Phoenix Mill · Stroud · Gloucestershire
in association with
Merthyr & Cynon Groundwork Trust
Fedw Hir · Llwydcoed · Aberdare · Mid Glamorgan

Second revised edition, 1996
Third revised edition, 1998

British Library Cataloguing in Publication Data

Vinter, Jeff
  Taff Trail: Official Guidebook
  I. Title
  914.2904

  ISBN 0–7509–0341–4

Library of Congress Cataloging-in-Publication Data applied for

Cover illustrations: top: *Talybont Reservoir viewed from near the foot of the Brecon & Merthyr Railway's Seven Mile Bank (author); bottom: an imposing view of Cefn Coed viaduct looking towards Merthyr Tydfil (David James Photography (Sussex)).*

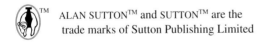 ALAN SUTTON™ and SUTTON™ are the
trade marks of Sutton Publishing Limited

Typeset in Times 9/11.
Typesetting and origination by
Sutton Publishing Limited.
Colour Separation by Yeo Valley.
Printed in Great Britain by
Ebenezer Baylis, Worcester.

CONTENTS

FOREWORD

BY TONY LEWIS

Chairman of the Wales Tourist Board

It is with great pleasure that I write this foreword to *The Taff Trail Official Guidebook*. The Wales Tourist Board is always delighted to see new facilities which can be enjoyed by visitors and residents alike. The Taff Trail takes you from the capital, Cardiff, through beautiful scenery in the Taff Valley into the grandeur of the Brecon Beacons, one of Wales's three National Parks. Your journey will take you at your own pace from Cardiff Bay, one of the most imaginative coastal redevelopment schemes of any city in Europe, through one of the former and famous coal mining valleys of South Wales to Merthyr Tydfil, where the Industrial Revolution was born. While you will see many interesting examples of Welsh Industrial Heritage, you will not fail to marvel at how the natural environment has been restored to its former beauty. I hope that you will enjoy the contents of this guide and will decide to walk or cycle along the Trail. I would like to congratulate the Merthyr and Cynon Groundwork Trust for their initiative in co-ordinating the work of so many in bringing the Trail into being.

TONY LEWIS

ACKNOWLEDGEMENTS

The Merthyr & Cynon Groundwork Trust (Executive Director Susan Price) is grateful to the officers and volunteers who have worked on the Trail, particularly Sue Bragg, Andrew Gray, Malcolm Hodgson, Chris Perks, Garry Stopp, Harley Thomas and Peter Williams. Many other organizations have participated in the Taff Trail Action Group. In addition to those mentioned in the Introduction which follows, thanks go to British Waterways, Cardiff Bay Development Corporation, the National Trust, the University of Glamorgan and the Welsh Office.

Andrew Gray, Pat Hart, David James, Kevin Littlewood, Pete Walker, Rhona White and Pete Wills assisted with general research for the book, and the author would like to thank Kevin Littlewood especially for his thorough and informative *Taff Trail Inventory*. Robert Turner and the staff of Winchester Library helped by tracing many of the canal, tramroad and railway histories used to provide the historical narratives in chapters 2 to 5. Mary Jones translated the Introduction into Welsh.

Many individuals and organizations helped with local enquiries, including Brecon Tourist Information Centre, British Waterways, Cardiff Bay Visitor Centre, City of Cardiff Leisure and Amenities Department, the Farmers' Union of Wales, Forest Enterprise, Glamorgan County Cricket Club, Merthyr Tydfil Tourist Information Centre, Pontypridd Town Council and the Welsh Rugby Union. The detailed information on local bus services was supplied by the public transport staff at Mid Glamorgan, South Glamorgan and Powys County Councils.

On a personal note, I would like to thank John Gibberd and David James, who assisted with photography and transport arrangements, often at unsociable hours. Their good company and willingness to help beyond all reasonable expectations was much appreciated. Finally, I must record my thanks to my wife, Jenny, who accepted the demands placed on our family life by yet another writing project. Her support for my efforts, and her tolerance of the paper mountain which engulfed parts of our home, were much appreciated.

JEFF VINTER

INTRODUCTION
What is the Taff Trail?

The Taff Trail is a long-distance recreational route in the form of a footpath and cycleway linking Cardiff and Brecon. The trail route illustrates the whole history of this area as it follows the course of the River Taff from Cardiff Bay on the Bristol Channel through one of the typical narrow industrialized Welsh coalfield valleys to Merthyr Tydfil, the nineteenth-century 'iron capital' of the world. North of Merthyr the trail passes through a dramatic change of scene as it leaves the industrialized valley behind and enters the Brecon Beacons National Park. The trail then rises steadily to its highest point as it crosses the watershed of the River Taff, before descending to the picturesque market town of Brecon in the fertile Usk

CYFLWYNIAD
Beth yw Llwybr Taf?

Llwybr hamdden hir yw Llwybr Taf ar ffurf llwybr troed a llwybr beiciau sy'n cysylltu Caerdydd ac Aberhonddu. Mae'r llwybr yn darlunio holl hanes yr ardal hon wrth ddilyn Afon Taf o Fae Caerdydd at Fôr Hafren drwy un o gymoedd glofaol cul nodweddiadol y de i Ferthyr Tudful, sef 'prifddinas haearn' y byd yn y bedwaredd ganrif ar bymtheg. I'r gogledd o Ferthyr mae'r llwybr yn newid yn llwyr wrth adael y cwm diwydiannol a mynd i mewn i Barc Cenedlaethol Bannau Brycheiniog. Wedyn mae'r llwybr yn codi'n gyson i'w fan uchaf wrth groesi cefndeuddwr Afon Taf, cyn disgyn eto i dref farchnad brydferth Aberhonddu yn nyffryn moethus Wysg. Mae'r llwybr tua 5 milltir o hyd ac yn

The peaks of the Brecon Beacons. The Taff Trail provides plenty of opportunity to explore this outstanding scenic area with its twin routes from Merthyr Tydfil to Brecon (Merthyr & Cynon Groundwork Trust)
Bannau Brycheiniog. Mae Llwybr Taf yn gyfle gwych i archwilio'r ardal hardd hon gyda'r ddwy ffordd o Ferthyr Tudful i Aberhonddu (Ymddiriedolaeth Groundwork Merthyr a Chynon)

Valley. It covers a distance of some 55 miles and utilizes canal towpaths, disused railways and tramroads which have been linked wherever possible to provide a safe and scenic route. Associated with the trail is a network of circular walks, cycle routes, bridleways, drives and picnic sites. The project's primary aim is to provide recreation for local communities and to attract tourists, visitors and sports enthusiasts to the Taff Valley. It was also intended to act as a catalyst to generate environmental improvement works in the valley as a whole.

The Development of the Taff Trail

The Taff Trail project was launched in September 1988 by the Rt Hon. Sir Wyn Roberts, MP. The project has been developed and coordinated by the Merthyr & Cynon Groundwork Trust, but over thirty organizations have actively supported the project, helped to steer it and participated with the Trust in its implementation. The key partners have been the counties and districts through which the trail passes, particularly Mid Glamorgan, South Glamorgan and Powys County Councils, Taff Ely, Merthyr Tydfil, Cynon Valley and Brecknock Borough Councils, Rhymney Valley District Council and Cardiff City Council; central government agencies, particularly the Countryside Council for Wales, the Welsh Development Agency, Forest Enterprise, the Wales Tourist Board, the Sports Council for Wales and British Rail; the Brecon Beacons National Park; other relevant organizations, particularly the Caerphilly Mountain Countryside Service, Merthyr Tydfil Heritage Trust, the Prince of Wales' Committee, Coed Cymru, Environment Wales, the Keep Wales Tidy Campaign and BTCV; community

defnyddio llwybrau tynnu wrth ymyl camlesi, hen reilffyrdd a thramffyrdd sydd wedi eu cysylltu, pryd bynnag y mae hynny'n bosibl, i greu llwybr diogel a hardd. Yn gysylltiedig â'r llwybr mae rhwydwaith o lwybrau troed mewn cylch, llwybrau beiciau, llwybrau ceffyl, ffyrdd gyrru a safleoedd picnic. Prif nod y cynllun yw darparu hamdden i gymunedau lleol a denu twristiaid, ymwelwyr a phobl sy'n hoffi chwaraeon i Ddyffryn Taf. Bwriadwyd i'r cynllun hefyd fod yn gatalydd i greu gwaith gwella yn y cwm yn gyffredinol.

Datblygiad Llwybr Taf

Lansiwyd cynllun Llwybr Taf ym mis Medi 1988 gan y Gwir Anrh Syr Wyn Roberts AS. Mae'r cynllun wedi ei ddatblygu a'i gydgysylltu gan Ymddiriedolaeth Groundtrust Merthyr a Chynon, ond mae dros ddeg ar hugain o gymdeithasau wedi rhoi cymorth ymarferol i'r cynllun, wedi helpu ei lywio a chymryd rhan gyda'r Ymddiriedolaeth yn ei weithredu. Y prif bartneriaid oedd y siroedd a'r dosbarthau y mae'r llwybr yn mynd drwy eu rhanbarthau, yn enwedig gynghorau sir Morgannwg Ganol, De Morgannwg a Phowys a chynghorau bwrdeistref Cwm Cynon a Brycheiniog, Cyngor Dosbarth Cwm Rhymni a Chyngor Dinas Caerdydd; asiantaethau'r llywodraeth ganolog, yn enwedig Gyngor Cefn Gwlad Cymru, Awdurdod Datblygu Cymru, y Fenter Coedwigoedd, Bwrdd Croeso Cymru, Cyngor Chwaraeon Cymru a'r Rheilffyrdd Prydeinig; Parc Cenedlaethol Bannau Brycheiniog; cyrff perthnasol eraill, yn enwedig Gwasanaeth Cefn Gwlad Mynydd Caerffili, Ymddiriedolaeth Etifeddiaeth Merthyr Tudful, Pwyllgor Tywysog Cymru, Coed Cymru, Amgylchedd Cymru, Ymgyrch Cadwch Gymru'n Daclus a'r Gwarchodwyr Cefn Gwlad; cyrff cymunedol; a'r sector organizations; and the private sector, particularly Sustrans Limited, Esso UK plc and Welsh Water.

The idea for the trail grew from work being undertaken by the Merthyr & Cynon Groundwork Trust in 1987 to improve footpath routes in its borough. The Trust is a charity undertaking environmental improvement work and the provision of countryside leisure and recreation facilities with local partners. Its work with the local authorities particularly showed the need to take a more strategic approach to recreation routes, to link existing facilities, to look at other long-distance routes and to consider wider environmental improvements. Cardiff City Council had already provided a cycle trail into the city, the Three Castles Cycle Route, while Taff Ely Borough was providing further cycle-route links in its area. Mid

preifat, yn enwedig Sustrans Cyf, Esso UK ccc a Dŵr Cymru.

Tyfodd y syniad o gael llwybr o'r gwaith a oedd yn cael ei wneud gan Ymddiriedolaeth Groundtrust Merthyr a Chynon ym 1987 i wella llwybrau ym Mwrdeistref Merthyr. Elusen yw'r Ymddiriedolaeth sy'n ymgymryd â gwaith gwella'r amgylchedd a darparu hamdden yng nghefn gwlad gyda phartneriaid lleol. Roedd ei waith gydag awdurdodau lleol yn dangos yn arbennig fod angen cael dull mwy strategol o ddelio â llwybrau hamdden, i gysylltu'r cyfleusterau personol, i edrych ar lwybrau hirfaith eraill ac ystyried gwelliannau ehangach i'r amgylchedd. Roedd Cyngor Dinas Caerdydd eisoes wedi darparu llwybr beiciau i mewn i'r ddinas, sef "Llwybr y Tri Chastell", ac roedd Cyngor Bwrdeistref Taf Elái yn darparu cysylltiadau pellach i feiciau o fewn

A number of new river crossings have been constructed including this new bridge over the river at Pwll Taf (Merthyr & Cynon Groundwork Trust)

Mae nifer o groesfannau newydd wedi eu codi dros yr afon, gan gynnwys y bont newydd hon ym Mhwll Taf (Ymddiriedolaeth Groundwork Merthyr a Chynon)

Glamorgan County Council had produced a document on the coordinated improvements needed in the Taff Valley, and the Brecon Beacons National Park was improving its network of recreational routes throughout the park area. None of these different initiatives really linked together, yet the Trust felt that the potential for recreational enjoyment through the more coordinated development of old tracks, industrial tramroads, disused railways, footpaths, forestry and minor roads was enormous, as was the scope for links to existing and new heritage centres and interpretation points, car parks and picnic sites.

It was with the issue of coordination in mind that the Groundwork Trust convened a seminar in 1988 to investigate the scope for a communal and coordinated approach to a trail and associated informal leisure provision in the Taff valleys and their catchment areas. The initiative was enthusiastically supported and led to the establishment of an action group to promote the development of the trail, chaired by the Trust. The project then obtained UK 2000 Cymru 'Flagship Project' status, which enabled a grant to be obtained for a project coordinator based with the Trust. A development plan was produced and agreed by the action group, and this provided the basis for a three-year programme of work that has made the trail a reality. Although each partner has contributed, a major part of the funding has come through Mid Glamorgan County Council accessing the Valleys Urban Programme. The actual works to the trail have been carried out primarily by the partners or contractors, but also by volunteers. Thanks particularly go to the volunteers from schools and community groups along the trail, who have waymarked it and other footpaths, planted trees, bulbs and hedges, cleared litter, put up fencing and gates, and led walks and cycle rides along it.

ei ranbarth. Roedd Cyngor Sir Morgannwg Ganol wedi cynhyrchu dogfen ar y gwelliannau cyd-gysylltu roedd eu hangen yn Nyffryn Taf, ac roedd Parc Cenedlaethol Bannau Brycheiniog yn gwella'i rwydwaith o lwybrau hamdden drwy'r parc i gyd. Doedd dim un o'r gwahanol fentrau hyn mewn gwirionedd yn cysylltu â'i gilydd, ac eto teimlai'r Ymddiriedolaeth fod yna gyfle gwych i fwynhau hamdden drwy ddatblygu'r hen draciau, y tramffyrdd diwydiannol, yr hen reilffyrdd, y llwybrau, y ffyrdd coedwigaeth a'r ffyrdd bach mewn ffordd fwy cysylltiedig, yn ogystal â'r cyfle gwych i gysylltu'r mannau treftadaeth presennol a rhai newydd, mannau dehongli, parciau ceir a safleoedd picnic.

Gyda'r syniad o gyd-gysylltu mewn golwg y galwodd Ymddiriedolaeth Goundtrust seminar ym 1988 i ymchwilio i bosibilrwydd cael dull cymunedol wedi ei gyd-gysylltu o greu llwybrau a darpariaethau hamdden anffurfiol cysylltiedig yng nghymoedd Taf a'u dalgylchoedd cysylltiedig. Cafodd y fenter gefnogaeth frwd ac arweiniodd at sefydlu grŵp eithredu i hybu datblygu'r llwybr, dan gadeiryddiaeth yr Ymddiriedolaeth. Wedyn rhoddwyd statws 'Cynllun Arwain' UK 2000 Cymru i'r cynllun, a olygai y gellid cael grant ar gyfer Cyd-gysylltydd Cynllun yn seiliedig o fewn yr Ymddiriedolaeth. Cafodd cynllun datblygu ei baratoi a'i gymeradwyo gan y grŵp gweithredu, ac roedd hwnnw'n sail ar gyfer rhaglen waith dair blynedd i ddod â'r llwybr i fodolaeth. Er bod pob un o'r partneriaid wedi cyfrannu, daeth rhan fawr o'r arian oddi wrth Gyngor Sir Morgannwg Ganol o'r Rhaglen Cymorth Trefol. Mae'r gwaith ei hun ar y llwybr wedi ei wneud yn bennaf gan y partneriaid neu'r contractwyr, ond hefyd gan wirfoddolwyr. Rhaid diolch yn arbennig i'r gwirfoddolwyr o ysgolion a grwpiau cymunedol ar hyd y llwybr, sydd wedi gosod arwyddion ar y llwybr hwn a llwybrau eraill, plannu coed,

The Groundwork Trust continues to employ a project coordinator to develop the future use of the trail and ensure its maintenance. A Taff Trail User Group of over fifty organizations has also been established.

The trail has been a truly collaborative project, a striking example of what can be achieved with commitment, enthusiasm and practical help from a wide range of organizations working together to achieve a common goal. We hope you enjoy it.

The Cycle Trail Movement

As noted above, the Taff Trail utilizes a considerable mileage of canal towpaths, disused railways and old tramroads. Trade and industry have always discarded old lines of communication when they are no longer required, and one need look no further than the supplanting of canals by railways and,

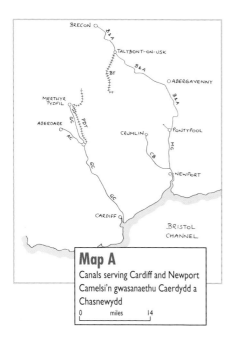

Map A

Canals serving Cardiff and Newport

Camelsi'n gwasanaethu Caerdydd a Chasnewydd

0   miles   14

bylbiau a chloddiau, clirio sbwriel, adeiladu ffensiau a gatiau, ac arwain teithiau ar ei hyd ar droed ac ar gefn beic. Mae Ymddiriedolaeth Groundwork yn parhau i gyflogi cydgysylltydd cynllun er mwyn datblygu defnyddio'r llwybr yn y dyfodol a sicrhau gofalu amdano. Mae Grŵp Defnyddwyr Llwybr Taf wedi ei lunio hefyd, sy'n cynnwys dros hanner cant o gymdeithasau.

Bu'r llwybr yn gynllun cydweithredol ym mhob ystyr, ac yn enghraifft wych o'r hyn y gellir ei wneud gydag ymroddiad, brwdfrydedd a chymorth ymarferol wrth i amrywiaeth helaeth o gyrff weithio gyda'i gilydd i gyrraedd un nod. Gobeithio y byddwch yn ei fwynhau.

Y Mudiad Llwybr Beiciau

Fel y nodwyd uchod, mae Llwybr Taf yn defnyddio milltiroedd lawer o lwybrau tynnu ar hyd camlesi, hen reilffyrdd a hen dramffyrdd. Mae masnach a diwydiant bob amser yn rhoi hen ddulliau cyfathrebu o'r neilltu pan na fydd eu hangen mwyach, a does dim angen edrych ymhellach na disodli'r camlesi gan reilffyrdd, ac yn fwy diweddar, ddisodli'r rheilffyrdd gan ffyrdd, er enghraifft. Yr hyn sy'n rhyfeddol, hwyrach, yw bod y naill genhedlaeth ar ôl y llall, tan yn ddiweddar, yn barod i adael yr hen lwybrau hyn bron yn union fel yr oedden nhw a heb eu defnyddio am ddegawdau ar y tro. Er enghraifft, roedd Camlas Morgannwg o Ferthyr Tudful i Gaerdydd wedi dod i ben i raddau helaeth erbyn troad y ganrif, ond ni

Abbreviations

AC	Aberdare Canal
B&A	Brecknock & Abergavenny Canal
BT	Brynoer Tramway
CB	Crumlin Branch of the Monmouthshire Canal
GC	Glamorganshire Canal
MC	Monmouthshire Canal
PDT	Pennydarren Tramway

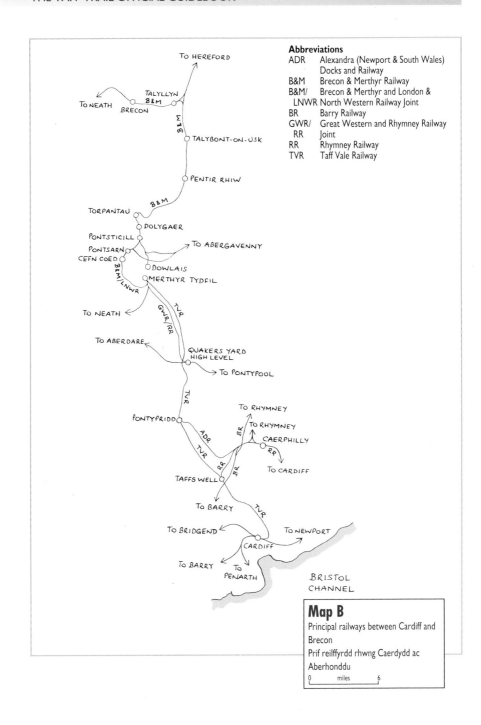

Abbreviations

ADR   Alexandra (Newport & South Wales)
        Docks and Railway
B&M   Brecon & Merthyr Railway
B&M/   Brecon & Merthyr and London &
LNWR   North Western Railway Joint
BR   Barry Railway
GWR/   Great Western and Rhymney Railway
  RR   Joint
RR   Rhymney Railway
TVR   Taff Vale Railway

TO HEREFORD

TO NEATH
TALYLLYN
B&M
BRECON

B&M

TALYBONT-ON-USK

PENTIR RHIW

B&M
TORPANTAU
DOLYGAER
PONTSTICILL
PONTSARN   TO ABERGAVENNY
CEFN COED
B&M/LNWR   DOWLAIS
        MERTHYR TYDFIL

TO NEATH

GWR/RR   TVR

TO ABERDARE
        QUAKERS YARD
        HIGH LEVEL
            TO PONTYPOOL

TVR

            TO RHYMNEY
PONTYPRIDD   TO RHYMNEY
        ADR   BR   CAERPHILLY
        TVR   RR   RR
            RR   BR   TO CARDIFF
TAFFS WELL   BR

        TVR
TO BARRY
TO BRIDGEND   TO NEWPORT
        CARDIFF
TO BARRY   TO
        PENARTH   BRISTOL
                       CHANNEL

Map B
Principal railways between Cardiff and
Brecon
Prif reilffyrdd rhwng Caerdydd ac
Aberhonddu

0   miles   6

more recently, railways by roads for examples. What is perhaps surprising is that, until recently, successive generations were prepared to leave these old routes largely intact and unused for decades at a time. For example, the Glamorganshire Canal from Merthyr Tydfil to Cardiff was largely moribund by the turn of the century, but was not obliterated by the new A470 dual carriageway until very recently.

One has to look at the recent history of the railways to understand how this casual attitude was changed. In the highly industrialized South Wales valleys, railways came and went with the industries they served and few paid any attention to the loss of a line deemed to have outlived its usefulness. There were periods of economy and contraction during the 1930s and 1950s, but railway closures really hit the headlines in 1963 when the innocently titled *Reshaping of British Railways* was published. This was the now infamous 'Beeching Report', which proposed that thousands of miles of railways be closed on a nationwide basis – a prescription designed to cure the industry's loss-making which, incidentally, the closures failed to achieve then as now. The result was a massive and unprecedented increase in the number of disused trackbeds littering the country and, by the end of the decade, the government was beginning to regard their continued dereliction as a source of mild concern.

The first official response to this appeared in 1970, when Dr J.H. Appleton, a reader in geography at Hull University, published a study entitled *Disused Railways in the Countryside of England and Wales*. For many, this was a disappointing document which did little more than chronicle the physical characteristics of the disused lines without suggesting any worthwhile new use for them. The next report, published in 1982, was entirely different. For this, the

chafodd ei dileu gan ffordd ddeuol yr A470 tan yn ddiweddar iawn.

Rhaid i ni edrych ar hanes diweddar y rheilffyrdd i ddeall sut y newidiodd yr agwedd ddidaro hon. Yng nghymoedd diwydiannol iawn De Cymru, byddai rheilffyrdd yn mynd ac yn dod gyda'r diwydiannau roedden nhw'n eu gwasanaethu, ac ychydig iawn fyddai'n rhoi llawer o sylw i gau llinell y byddai pobl yn barnu ei bod wedi dod i ddiwedd ei hoes ddefnyddiol. Gwelwyd cyfnodau o leihau a chrebachu yn ystod y 1930au a'r 1950au, ond yr hyn a dynnodd y sylw mwyaf at gau rheilffyrdd oedd cyhoeddi adroddiad dan y teitl diniwed *Reshaping of British Railways* ym 1963. Hwnnw oedd yr 'Adroddiad Beeching' enwog, a gynigiai gau miloedd o filltiroedd o reilffyrdd ar hyd a lled y wlad - cynllun i roi terfyn ar golledion y diwydiant, ond methiant fu'r cau bryd hynny fel heddiw. Y canlyniad oedd cynnydd eithriadol na welwyd ei debyg yn nifer y cledrau diffaith ar hyd a lled y wlad, ac erbyn diwedd y degawd, roedd y llywodraeth yn dechrau gofidio ychydig am y dadfeilio parhaus.

Cafwyd yr ymateb swyddogol cyntaf i hyn ym 1970 pan gyhoeddodd Dr J.H. Appleton, darllenydd mewn daearyddiaeth ym Mhrifysgol Hull, astudiaeth o dan y teitl *Disused Railways in the Countryside of England and Wales*. I lawer, dogfen siomedig oedd honno, yn gwneud fawr iawn mwy na chrynhoi nodweddion ffisegol yr hen reilffyrdd heb awgrymu unrhyw ffordd newydd, fuddiol i'w defnyddio. Roedd yr adroddiad nesaf, ym 1982, yn hollol wahanol. Ar gyfer hwnnw, comisiynodd yr Adran Drafnidiaeth gwmni o ymgynghorwyr peirianneg sifil, John Grimshaw a'r Cymdeithion, i ymdrin â'r un broblem. Ymatebodd Grimshaw gydag adroddiad canolog o dan y teitl *A Study of Disused Railways in England and Wales*, yn cael ei gefnogi gan ddim llai na thri ar ddeg ar hugain o 'atodiadau' ar wahân.

Department of Transport commissioned a firm of civil engineering consultants, John Grimshaw and Associates, to address the same problem. Grimshaw responded with a central report entitled *A Study of Disused Railways in England and Wales*, backed by no less than thirty-three separate 'annexes'.

Grimshaw was, and remains, a man with a mission. An avid cyclist keenly aware of the dangers faced by cyclists on increasingly busy public roads, he proposed that disused railways be used to create a network of off-road cycling and walking routes. His thirty-three annexes showed in detail how these conversions could be achieved economically and effectively in a variety of different locations throughout the United Kingdom. A short time later he set up a charitable company, Sustrans Limited ('sustainable transport'), to convert a disused railway line between Bath and Bristol into a purpose-built cycle trail linking the two cities. The first section of this opened in 1986 and was an instant success. Within five years it had been extended to link the two cities and, when surveyed recently, was estimated to be generating about one million journeys per annum, split equally between walkers and cyclists.

This level of use demonstrates that people will actually cycle in large numbers where there are safe facilities to do so. At the time of writing there are hundreds of local cycling schemes throughout England and Wales, and Sustrans is now working on linking them together via long-distance routes such as the Trans-Pennine Trail (Hull to Liverpool). John Grimshaw's current ambition is to secure 1 per cent of the nation's road-building budget for the construction of new cycling schemes. Recent Department of Transport statistics, showing that 75 per cent of all journeys are for 5 miles or less, indicate that the bicycle could be used far more as a cheap and efficient means of personal transport.

Dyn gyda gweledigaeth oedd Grimshaw bryd hynny, ac mae'n parhau felly. Roedd yn feiciwr brwd ac yn ymwybodol iawn o beryglon beicwyr ar ffyrdd cyhoeddus a oedd yn mynd yn fwyfwy prysur. Cynigiodd y dylai'r hen reilffyrdd gael eu defnyddio i greu rhwydwaith o lwybrau beicio a cherdded o gyrraedd y ffyrdd. Roedd ei dri ar ddeg ar hugain o atodiadau'n dangos yn fanwl sut y gellid eu haddasu'n economaidd ac yn effeithiol mewn nifer o wahanol fannau ar hyd a lled y Deyrnas Gyfunol. Ychydig yn ddiweddarach, sefydlodd gwmni elusennol, Sustrans Cyfyngedig (am 'sustainable transport') i droi hen reilffordd rhwng Caerfaddon a Bryste yn llwybr beiciau pwrpasol i gysylltu'r ddwy ddinas. Agorwyd y rhan gyntaf ym 1986 a bu'n llwyddiant ar unwaith. Cyn pen pum mlynedd roedd wedi ei ymestyn i gysylltu'r ddwy ddinas, a phan wnaed arolwg yno'n ddiweddar, amcangyfrifiwyd bod y llwybr yn creu tua miliwn o deithiau y flwyddyn, yn cael eu rhannu'n gyfartal rhwng cerddwyr a beicwyr.

Mae'r niferoedd hyn yn dangos bod llawer iawn o bobl yn barod i feicio lle bydd cyfleusterau diogel i wneud hynny. Wrth ysgrifennu hwn, mae yna gannoedd o gynlluniau beicio lleol ar hyd Cymru a Lloegr, ac mae Sustrans nawr yn gweithio ar gynllun i'w cysylltu ar hyd llwybrau hirfaith fel y Llwybr ar draws y Pennines (Hull i Lerpwl). Uchelgais presennol John Grimshaw yw sicrhau bod un y cant o gyllideb y wlad ar gyfer adeiladu ffyrdd yn mynd ar adeiladu cynlluniau beicio newydd. Mae ystadegau diweddar yr Adran Drafnidiaeth, sy'n dangos bod 75 y cant o'r holl siwrneiau sy'n cael eu gwneud yn bum milltir neu lai, yn awgrymu y gallai'r beic gael ei ddefnyddio lawer yn fwy fel math rhad ac effeithlon o gludiant personol.

This, then, is the general context within which the Taff Trail should be seen. Given that much of the route lies within the Brecon Beacons National Park, it naturally has a strong leaning towards leisure and tourism, but in Cardiff there are already cycling commuters who use the trail in preference to other modes of transport to reach their places of work. Other cycling routes in South Wales are already at or beyond the planning stage (see Appendix D). The success of the Taff Trail should provide them all with a healthy boost.

How to Use the Guide

The guide has been written in a northerly direction, from Cardiff to Brecon, on the assumption that a majority of trail users will arrive at Cardiff as a result of its excellent transport links with the rest of the country. The whole of the main route is equally suitable for both cyclists and walkers, but between Cefn-Coed-y-Cymmer and Brecon there is an alternative mountain route via Storey Arms. This is described in a *southerly* direction in order to return Trail users to Merthyr Tydfil, where there are again good rail connections.

The mountain route was originally designed for walkers only, although it has always been possible for cyclists to follow it from Brecon to the A470 at Storey Arms. However, the recent introduction of a cycle-hire facility at Garwnant has led to the establishment of a new cycling route from there southwards to Cefn Coed, where the main cycleway may be joined. In future, it is possible that an off-road cycling route will be established between Storey Arms and Garwnant as well.

Many walkers and cyclists will find it helpful to use the guide in conjunction with the relevant Ordnance Survey maps and, to

Dyma'r cyd-destun cyffredinol, felly, i ystyried Llwybr Taf. O gofio bod rhan helaeth o'r llwybr o fewn ffiniau Parc Cenedlaethol Bannau Brycheiniog, mae'n tueddu'n naturiol tuag at hamdden a thwristiaeth. Ond yng Nghaerdydd, mae yna gymudwyr beicio sydd eisoes yn defnyddio'r llwybr yn lle mathau eraill o gludiant i fynd at eu gwaith. Mae llwybrau beicio eraill yn Ne Cymru sydd eisoes ar y gweill neu wedi eu cynllunio (gweler Atodiad D). Dylai llwyddiant Llwybr Taf fod yn hwb iachus i bob un ohonynt.

Sut i Ddefnyddio'r Arweiniad

Mae'r arweiniad wedi ei ysgrifennu tua'r gogledd, o Gaerdydd i Aberhonddu, gan dybied y bydd y mwyafrif o bobl sy'n defnyddio'r llwybr yn cyrraedd Caerdydd oherwydd y cysylltiadau cludiant gwych â gweddill y wlad. Mae'r prif lwybr lawn mor addas i feicwyr a cherddwyr fel ei gilydd, ond rhwng Cefncoedycymer ac Aberhonddu mae yna lwybr mynydd ar wahân drwy Storey Arms (gweler pennod 6). Mae hwnnw'n addas i gerddwyr yn unig ac y mae wedi ei ysgrifennu tua'r de er mwyn dod â'r teithwyr nôl i Ferthyr Tudful, lle mae yna gysylltiadau rheilffordd da. Gan fod cyfleusterau hurio beiciau wedi dechrau yng Ngarwnant, mae trefniadau'n cael eu gwneud i alluogi pobl i feicio oddi yno tua'r de i Gefn-coed ac ymuno â'r prif lwybr beiciau.

Bydd llawer o gerddwyr yn ei chael yn fuddiol defnyddio'r arweiniad ar y cyd â'r mapiau Arolwg Ordnans perthnasol, ac i'r diben hwnnw caiff cyfeiriadau grid chwe ffigur eu darparu drwy'r llyfr i gyd. Dyma rifau'r tudalennau perthnasol:

Graddfa 1:25,000 : Tudalennau Landranger
160, 161, 170 ac 171

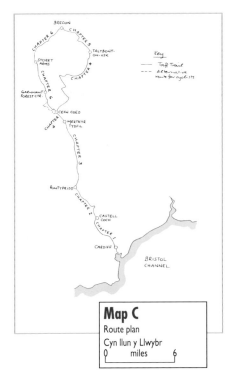

Map C
Route plan
Cyn llun y Llwybr
0   miles   6

Graddfa 1:50,000 :   Map Outdoor Leisure
11 (Bannau Brychein-
iog)
Tudalennau Pathfinder
1109, 1129, 1148 ac
1165

Yn yr achos hwn, mae'n werth cael y tudalennau 1:50,000 sy'n dangos y llwybr yn y canol.

Mae'r llwybr wedi ei gynllunio fel llwybr llinellol hirfaith a disgwylir y bydd llawer o deithwyr yn ei ddefnyddio felly. Gellir beicio ar ei hyd mewn diwrnod, ond bydd dau neu dri diwrnod yn rhoi'r amser ychwanegol sydd eisiau i ymweld â rhai o'r atyniadau gerllaw. Ni ddylai fod yn anodd i gerddwyr deithio ar hyd y prif lwybr yn gyfan mewn tri i bum diwrnod, yn ôl eu profiad a'u cyflymdra. Cofiwch roi diwrnod cyfan yn ychwanegol os bwriadwch gynnwys y llwybr mynydd drwy Storey Arms. Yn gyffredinol, bydd beiciwr sy'n weddoll ffit yn teithio yn ôl tua 15mya a cherddwr lled ffit yn ôl tua 3mya.

Os byddwch chi'n cerdded y llwybr yn gyfan, h.y. Caerdydd - Merthyr Tudful - Cefn-coed - Tal-y-bont - Aberhonddu - Storey Arms - Cefn-coed - Merthyr Tudful, ni chewch fawr o ffwdan cael cludiant cyhoeddus, gan fod gwasanaeth rheilffordd da yng Nghaerdydd a Merthyr. Ond bydd angen ychydig mwy o drefnu ar gyfer teithiau cerdded llinellau byrrach. Mae'n bosibl mynd gyda ffrindiau a defnyddio dau gar, gan adael un ym mhob pen o'r adran a ddewisiwch, ond fe all y gwasanaeth bysiau - yn enwedig o'r de i Ferthyr - fod lawn mor gyfleus; efallai'n fwy cyfleus am na fyddwch yn gwastraffu amser yn trefnu'r ceir. Yn Atodiad A mae crynodeb cynhwysfawr o'r gwasanaethau sydd ar gael, er ei bod bob amser yn ddoeth gwneud yn siŵr o'r man-ylion naill ai gyda'r gweithredwyr eu hunain neu swyddfa cludiant cyhoeddus y cyngor sir

this end, six-figure grid references are supplied throughout the book. The relevant sheet numbers are as follows:

Scale 1:50,000 :   Landranger sheets 160,
161, 170 and 171
Scale 1:25,000 :   Outdoor Leisure Map 11
(Brecon Beacons)
Pathfinder sheets 1109,
1129, 1148 and 1165

In this case, it really is worth obtaining the 1:50,000 sheets which show the trail centrally.

The trail has been designed as a long-distance linear route and it is expected that many users will follow it as such. It can be cycled in a day, but two or three days will provide the extra time needed to explore some of the nearby attractions. Walkers should have no difficulty in covering the main trail in three to five days, depending on experience and pace. Allow an extra full day if you intend to include the mountain route via Storey Arms. As a general guide, a moderately fit cyclist averages 15 mph and a moderately fit walker 3 mph.

If you are walking the entire route, i.e. Cardiff–Merthyr Tydfil–Cefn Coed–Talybont–Brecon–Storey Arms–Cefn Coed–Merthyr Tydfil, public transport presents little difficulty as both Cardiff and Merthyr are well served by rail. However, shorter linear walks require a little more planning. It may be possible to go with friends and use two cars, when one can be left at each end of the chosen section, but the bus services – particularly south of Merthyr – can be equally convenient; perhaps more so, as no time is wasted in deploying cars. Appendix A provides a comprehensive summary of the services available, although it is wise to check details with either the operators themselves or the relevant county council public transport office. Bus services are now 'deregulated' and can change at alarmingly short notice. As a general guide, do the bus journey first, then you will always be walking 'back to base'. For cyclists, the problem can be solved easily by cycling both ways: the views are surprisingly different in the opposite direction.

No attempt has been made to predict how long a particular section of the walk will take, as this is dependent on many variable factors such as age, fitness, experience, etc. Instead, individual chapters are described as '7 miles, easy', '17 miles, energetic', and so on. 'Easy' means that the route is completely flat and easy to complete in one go, whereas 'energetic' means that it is long, includes some appreciable gradients and may have short sections with a rough surface.

Most of the trail has a dry, smooth surface, although the towpath of the perthnasol. Mae gwasanaethau bysiau wedi eu dad-reoleiddio erbyn hyn a gall eu trefniadau newid yn eithriadol o gyflym. Yn gyffredinol, ewch ar y bws i ddechrau, yna fe fyddwch bob amser yn cerdded yn ôl i'r man cychwyn. I feicwyr, gall y broblem gael ei datrys yn hawdd drwy feicio i'r ddau gyfeiriad: gall y golygfeydd fod yn wahanol iawn i'r cyfeiriad arall.

Ni wnaed unrhyw ymgais i ragweld pa mor hir fydd rhan arbennig o'r daith yn ei gymryd, oherwydd mae hynny'n dibynnu ar nifer o ffactorau sy'n gallu amrywio, megis oed, ffitrwydd, profiad, ac yn y blaen. Yn lle hynny, disgrifir y gwahanol benodau fel '7 milltir, hawdd', '17 milltir, egniol', ac yn y blaen. Mae 'Hawdd' yn golygu bod y daith yn hollol wastad ac yn hawdd ei gorffen mewn un siwrnai, ond mae 'egniol' yn golygu bod y daith yn hir, yn cynnwys rhai llethrau sylweddol a gall rhai adrannau byr fod yn arw.

Mae wyneb y llwybr am y rhan fwyaf o'r daith yn llyfn ac yn sych, er yn gall y llwybr tynnu wrth ymyl Camlas Aberhonddu fod ychydig yn lleidiog yn y gaeaf. Mae hynny'n golygu nad oes raid i chi wisgo esgidiau gorymdeithio na chot pysgotwr. Ond byddwch yn gall: os byddwch chi'n mynd i ben y mynyddoedd, cofiwch fod y tywydd yn gallu newid yn gyflym ac y gall fod yn eithriadol o oer a glwyb - hyd yn oed yn yr haf. Os nad ydych chi'n siŵr, gallwch gel rhagolygon y tywydd yn lleol ar y rhifau teleffon canlynol, sy'n rhoi gwybodaeth 24-awr wedi ei recordio am y tywydd gan y Swyddfa Dywydd:

Morgannwg	0891 500409
Powys	0891 500414

Mae digon o arwyddion ar y llwybr, felly fe ddylai fod yn anodd i chi fynd ar goll, er bod fandaliaid weithiau'n creu problemau drwy ddinistrio byrddau lleol. Mae yna un

Monmouthshire and Brecon Canal can be rather boggy during the winter. This means that one does not necessarily have to wear marching boots and sou'westers. However, do be sensible: if you are going up on to the mountains, please remember that the weather can change rapidly, and that it can be bitingly cold and damp – even during the summer. If in doubt, you can obtain local weather forecasts from the following telephone numbers, which provide a 24-hour service of recorded weather information provided by the Meteorological Office:

Glamorgan   0891 500409
Powys   0891 500414

The trail is well waymarked, so it should be difficult to get lost, although vandals occasionally create problems by destroying local finger boards. There are one or two places where a vandalized sign could easily lead to a missed turning, so keep an eye on the map and look out for other waymarking signs like the yellow circles of paint applied to the trees in the woods south of Cantref Reservoir. As a general word of advice, nowhere does the trail reach the ridge of the local mountains, so if you find yourself here, you *have* gone wrong and should try to make your way down into the valley. If in any doubt, aim for the nearest road – the A470 on the mountain route via Storey Arms, or the lane from Pontsticill to Talybont on the main trail via Torpantau.

If you plan your journey carefully and give yourself plenty of time to complete it, you should not experience any difficulty. In an age driven increasingly by the need to rush and save time, there is much to be said for taking the Taff Trail at your leisure. Give yourself time to enjoy the countryside through which it passes, read about its history in this guide, and explore some of its many historic sites.

neu ddau fan lle gallai arwyddion sydd wedi eu fandaleiddio olygu colli tro, felly cadwch lygad ar y map a chwiliwch am arwyddion marcio eraill fel y cylchoedd o baent melyn ar y coed i'r de o Gronfa Ddŵr Cantref. A gair o gyngor cyffredinol. Dydy'r llwybr ddim yn mynd yn agos i ymyl y mynyddoedd lleol o gwbl, felly os gwelwch eich bod wedi cyrraedd yno, fe fyddwch yn sicr wedi colli'ch ffordd, a dylech geisio gwneud eich ffordd i lawr i'r dyffryn. Os byddwch yn ansicr, anelwch at y ffordd agosaf - yr A470 ar gyfer y ffordd gerdded drwy Storey Arms, neu'r lôn o Bontsticill i Dal-y-bont ar y prif lwybr drwy Dorpantau.

Os trefnwch eich taith yn ofalus a chymryd digon o amser i'w gorffen, ni ddylech gael unrhyw anhawster. Mewn oes o ruthro cynyddol ac arbed amser, mae yna lawer i'w ddweud dros deithio ar hyd Llwybr Taf yn eich pwysau. Rhowch amser i chi'ch hun fwynhau'r wlad y mae'r llwybr yn mynd drwyddi. Darllenwch amdani yn yr aweiniad hwn ac ewch i weld rhai o'i llu safleoedd hanesyddol.

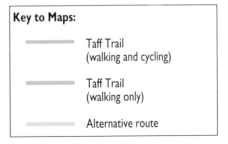

Key to Maps:

Taff Trail
(walking and cycling)

Taff Trail
(walking only)

Alternative route

The northern terminus of the Monmouthshire and Brecon Canal at Brecon. The trail uses part of the nineteenth-century Brynoer Tramway to reach Talybont-on-Usk, where it switches to the towpath of this historic and attractive waterway (David James Photography (Sussex))

'The Ring' by Harvey Hood, Head of Sculpture at Cardiff Institute of Higher Education, was commissioned by Cardiff Bay Development Corporation and occupies a prominent site overlooking the Inner Harbour, Cardiff Bay. It forms the starting point for the Taff Trail in Cardiff and includes details cast in bronze to suggest the past and future of the Bay (Cardiff Bay Development Corporation)

I

CARDIFF TO CASTELL COCH

THREE CASTLES

7 MILES
EASY
ORDNANCE
SURVEY MAPS
1:50,000 Landranger
sheet 171
1:25,000 Pathfinder
Sheets 1148 and 1165

Introduction

Between Cardiff and Castell Coch, the Taff Trail shares the course of the Three Castles Cycle Route. This currently runs from Cardiff Castle to Nantgarw, north of Castell Coch, and will one day be extended to Caerphilly via Penrhos cutting on the Rhymney Railway's disused Taff's Well–Caerphilly branch. Anyone who thinks that all castles are fundamentally the same would be well advised to visit Cardiff Castle and Castell Coch. Both bear the stamp of the 3rd Marquis of Bute and his architect, William Burges, who fashioned them as flamboyant re-creations of the Middle Ages.

Cardiff is a very green city, as revealed by this aerial view of the civic centre. It has recently been judged one of the four best cities in Great Britain (City of Cardiff Leisure and Amenities Department)

Cardiff itself is a city full of character and history, and the Taff Trail passes many sites of interest. A recent national survey has judged it to be one of the four best cities in Great Britain. Apart from excellent shopping facilities and a wide range of tourist attractions, it also has a generous quota of parks and gardens, which are lavishly stocked with flowers. The displays of bulbs in March and April are second to none.

To the north of the city the trail follows the course of the River Taff wherever possible, passing close by historic Llandaff with its beautifully restored cathedral. At Whitchurch the industrial aspect of the trail becomes apparent where it utilizes part of the old Melingriffith Tramway, although one would be hard-pressed nowadays to recognize that this attractive green lane was once an industrial railway. Part of the abandoned Glamorganshire Canal lies nearby: just under a mile of this famous navigation is still in water, and is now managed as an aquatic nature reserve. Nearby stands the restored Melingriffith water pump, a miraculous survival from 1807, which is considered to be one of the most important industrial monuments in Europe.

The trail then slips unnoticed beneath the M4 and A470 roads to reach the village of Tongwynlais, which used to be the junction of the Merthyr and Cardiff turnpikes. A short climb up the lane to Caerphilly Common leads to Castell Coch, the Victorian 'fantasy castle'. This extraordinary, triple-turreted extravagance is illuminated at night and clearly visible from the nearby A470.

Route Description

Note: Additional routes between Cardiff Bay and the Cardiff central area are being investigated as a part of the ongoing redevelopment of the area. These will be signposted as and when they are constructed. Where there is a choice of alternative routes this is indicated by numbering in directions.

(1) Cardiff Bay to Western Avenue, Llandaff

The Taff Trail begins at Bute West dock basin (GR 193745), where Harvey Hood's sculpture *The Ring* has been installed as a landmark. From here, proceed west along Stuart Street and turn right into Adelaide Street. Pass Adelaide Place on the left, then turn left at the crossroads into Clarence Road. Follow Clarence Road over the River Taff, then turn right just after the river bridge to pick up a new section of trail along the west bank of the river.

Harvey Hood's sculpture was commissioned to create a striking and attractive feature at the start of the trail. It is made from bronze which is polished on the

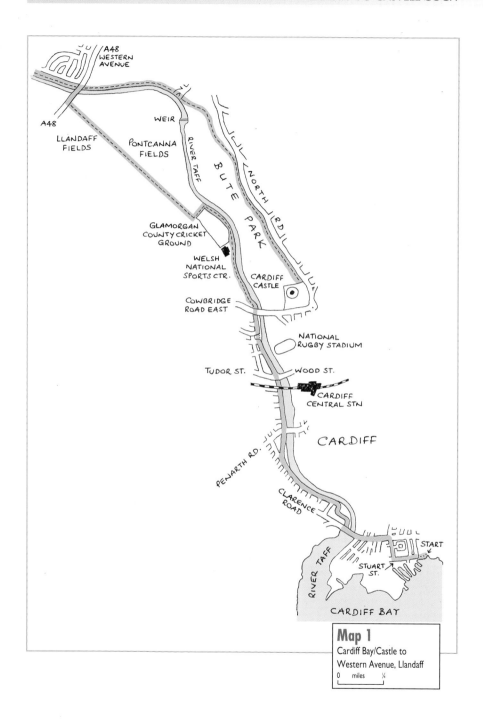

Map 1
Cardiff Bay/Castle to
Western Avenue, Llandaff

0   miles   ¼

outside and patinated deep blue and green on the inside. The idea is to focus visitors' attention on the panorama visible from the start of the trail. The sculpture is extremely strong and impervious to the elements; it is also designed to withstand several drunks climbing on it!

The docks at Cardiff have a long history. The first sea lock and basin were opened in June 1798 as part of the Glamorganshire Canal (see Chapter 3). However, most of the development was undertaken by the 2nd Marquis of Bute (1793–1848), who profited massively from the enterprise: not only did he own most of the land on which the docks were built, he also owned large mineral rights inland. As a result, many colliery and ironworks' owners found themselves in the grip of a double monopoly, which led to frequent complaints of high charges and poor access. When the Taff Vale Railway opened in 1841, delays in returning empty railway wagons became another sore point. Despite steady expansion at Cardiff from 1839 to 1887, the situation did not really ease until rival docks had been created at Ely tidal harbour, Penarth and Barry. With the benefit of hindsight, it can be seen that the real problem was the 'embarrassment of riches' flowing down the valleys for export. Between 1840 and 1900 the exports handled at Cardiff increased from 46,042 to 10,300,000 tons, so it is perhaps not surprising that the Bute Trustees had difficulty keeping pace with demand.

In recent years industrial decline has been the problem, with the docks area becoming run down and, in places, derelict. The response to this has been the establishment of the Cardiff Bay Development Corporation, which is responsible for leading the regeneration of the area over the coming years. The result is one of the largest regeneration schemes in Europe: the site comprises 2,700 acres of land which will witness the construction of 6,000 new homes and 9 million square feet of commercial and industrial space. The corporation is committed to the highest standards of design and plans to build to a 'human' scale; it sees one of its main objectives as 're-uniting the city and its waterfront'. There is a permanent free exhibition in the Cardiff Bay Visitor Centre, which is situated on the waterfront just east of the start of the trail. The building cannot be missed as it looks like a long tube on stilts.

While in the Cardiff Bay area, there is much else to see. Given the setting, many of the features have an industrial flavour, none more so than the Welsh Industrial and Maritime Museum with its associated Railway Gallery. These tell how Cardiff expanded over two centuries to become one of the world's largest ports. While on the subject of industrial history, it is worth having a look at some of the magnificent buildings in the area: the Coal Exchange in James Street was once the coal-dealing centre of Britain, while the imposing red-brick Pierhead Building is still in use as the offices of Cardiff docks. Techniquest in Stuart Street offers a 'hands on' experience of science and technology, while Q-Shed on the other side of the road contains a frequently changing exhibition on the area's history. However, the most surprising building on the waterfront is arguably the reconstruction of a Norwegian church, which is a short walk beyond the tube-like visitor centre. This commemorates the place where author Roald Dahl was baptized.

> The riverside path soon joins Taff Embankment, which follows the river as far as Penarth Road (GR 180755). At Penarth Road, continue straight ahead into Taff's Mead Embankment, passing under the western end of Cardiff Central station at GR 179758. Cross Wood Street via a 'toucan' crossing and continue straight ahead into Fitzhamon Embankment; where this road turns sharp left into Dispenser Street, carry straight on along the river bank, passing a pub on your left. In a few yards you will be in Coldstream Terrace, which should be followed to its junction with Cowbridge Road East, the main road past Cardiff Castle.

In the days of the Great Western Railway, Cardiff station used to be known as Cardiff General. A station has stood on this site since 1850, the present one dating from GWR rebuilding in 1932. To the untrained eye the station still looks busy, but modern traffic is about half of that handled in the mid-1950s; in those days, between 6 a.m. and 10 p.m. a passenger train arrived or departed every three to four minutes. At peak periods in the summer the station would be jammed to capacity with holiday-makers and day-trippers as railway staff struggled to manage the many timetable alterations and additions which applied on such occasions. One former employee recalls how the chaos was considerably worsened one Saturday in August 1956 when a young boy, bored by the long wait for his train, started to operate the train departure bell, his random codes being relayed to confused staff in Cardiff West signal-box.

A short distance beyond the station, the trail passes Cardiff Arms Park, the Welsh national rugby ground, which stands on the opposite bank of the Taff. Rugby has been played on this site for over a century, the first international taking place on 12 April 1884. However, for much of its life the site was shared with Cardiff Athletic Club and a greyhound-racing company, which made it impossible to develop the ground solely for rugby. The problem of joint ownership and use was not fully resolved until the mid-1970s. The present ground was developed between 1967 and 1984 at a cost of nearly £9 million, the vast majority of this being raised by the game itself through clubs and club members. Such is the popularity of rugby union that none of the debenture issues were undersubscribed. Without this degree of support and commitment, the redevelopment scheme might well have foundered: the Welsh Rugby Union was told initially that the total cost of its plans would be only £2¼ million.

> On reaching Cowbridge Road East, continue straight ahead into Sophia Gardens, keeping to the west bank of the river as far as the northern end of Glamorgan County Cricket Ground (GR 173773). At this point turn left, proceed straight ahead for 150 yd and turn right on reaching a long avenue of trees. This is the main path across Pontcanna Fields, which should be followed past a caravan park and television studios (both on the left) as far as Western Avenue, Llandaff (GR 161782). At this point turn right, cross the river bridge and, on the east bank of the river, turn left onto the main trail to Castell Coch.

The attractive Sophia Gardens were originally owned by the Bute family, who donated them to the city. The extent of the family's property in Cardiff reveals the size of the fortune it made in the nineteenth century. The trail passes behind the Welsh National Sports Centre, which can be seen on the left. This was opened by Princess Anne in June 1972 and has an excellent range of facilities, including a shooting range, swimming pool, squash courts and weight-lifting facilities. It is open to members only, but there are good arrangements for spectators.

The Glamorgan County Cricket Ground is situated immediately beyond the National Sports Centre on a site rented from Cardiff Cricket Club, which moved here from Cardiff Arms Park in 1967. Glamorgan County Cricket Club was formed in 1888 and spent its early years in minor-county cricket. It became the seventeenth member of the First Class County Championship in 1921, when it succeeded in finding eight other clubs willing to guarantee home and away fixtures. During the summer there is usually a county match at the ground every few days and, at other times, there are games in the various local leagues.

(2) Cardiff Castle to Western Avenue, Llandaff

> The original Cardiff section of the Taff Trail starts at GR 180768, just north of Cardiff Castle. Nowadays this is Castle Mews car park, which is probably the longest and thinnest car park in the whole city. Its peculiar dimensions are accounted for by the fact that it was originally part of the Glamorganshire Canal. The car park and cycle trail run alongside the A470 past the ambulance station at GR 175776. The trail then skirts the northern edge of Bute Park, passing an attractive park-keeper's lodge at GR 169782.
>
> Beyond the keeper's lodge there are two cycle trails running in parallel; follow the route on the left. This runs alongside the east bank of the Taff and passes under Western Avenue at GR 161783.

Cardiff Castle is actually many castles in one. The oldest remains are sections of wall which date from the third Roman fort on the site; the keep, which occupies a dominant position on a steep-sided mound, was built in the twelfth century to

Cardiff Castle includes sections of Roman, Norman and medieval origin, but the 3rd Marquis of Bute added the embellishments and ornate clock tower seen here. His aim was to produce a romantic re-creation of the Middle Ages. The interior is even more extravagant than the exterior (author)

replace an earlier timber fortification; while the Black Tower is part of a new castle started in the thirteenth century. The character of the castle began to change in about 1774, when Henry Holland started work on a castellated mansion with grounds laid out by Capability Brown. However, this was nothing compared with the alterations carried out by the 3rd Marquis of Bute, who with his architect, William Burges, set about turning it into a romantic re-creation of the Middle Ages. At the time the marquis was reputed to be the richest man in the world and the extravagance of his creation has to be seen to be believed. Even occasional rooms, such as the Summer Smoking Room, are embellished with statues, murals, candelabra, gold, silver, copper and brass.

North of the castle the trail follows the course of the Glamorganshire Canal as far as the park-keeper's lodge at GR 169783. Along the way it runs past the back of The Canal Boat public house in North Road, which confirms the waterway connection. As noted above, the trail swings left by the lodge but the course of the canal can be followed for another half mile as far as Gabalfa, where its route is occupied by housing. The canal bed is now a narrow tarmacked lane lined with overhanging trees; only these and the lane's dimensions give any clue as to its history.

The entrance to the Bishop's Palace at Llandaff, now open as a public garden. The imposing gatehouse survives, although much of the main building has been destroyed (David James Photography (Sussex))

The canal's route south of the castle is also of interest. The pedestrian subway under Kingsway, which runs alongside the castle's east wall, is an original canal bridge complete with a short section of towpath. Beyond this, the canal burrowed under Queen Street via a gaslit 115 yd tunnel, which probably still survives in the cellars of local department stores. The remainder of the route is above ground and can be traced on a street map via East Canal Wharf, Canal Parade and the public open space leading to Clarence Road.

Back at Western Avenue, a short diversion off the Taff Trail leads to Llandaff, where the cathedral and restored remains of the Bishop's Palace will be found. Llandaff has been a religious centre since the sixth century, when St Teilo established a monastery here. The present cathedral was founded in Norman times and completed by about 1500, but it suffered much subsequent neglect. During the Civil War, Parliamentary troops used it as an alehouse and, later still, it was used as a cattle pen and post office. Restoration took place during the eighteenth and nineteenth centuries, but further damage occurred in 1941 when a German land mine exploded on the site. This demolished much of the southern wall, necessitating further rebuilding which was completed in 1958.

The obvious route to the cathedral, via Western Avenue, is extremely busy and is not recommended. A safer and more attractive alternative is to follow the riverside path on the west bank of the Taff as far as GR 155783 and there turn left across the playing fields; this leads past the western end of the cathedral, which can be seen nestling among trees on the hillside. Cyclists are asked to walk this section as it is a footpath rather than a cycleway. If you are looking for refreshments, it is worth turning the corner by the Bishop's Palace into Llandaff High Street, where the Black Lion will be found – a traditional Brain's pub offering both real ale and food.

A view of the southern elevation of Llandaff Cathedral. In 1941 a German land mine exploded here, necessitating extensive rebuilding. The new stonework reveals the scale of the damage (David James Photography (Sussex))

Western Avenue, Llandaff to Castell Coch

North of Western Avenue the trail follows the east bank of the Taff as far as GR 145793, where it turns sharp right. It then runs across the southern end of a playing field for 150 yd before turning sharp left at the end of Old Radyr Road (GR 145793). It then runs north for 300 yd, turning left on reaching Ty Mawr Road. In a matter of yards it passes under a railway bridge on the Cardiff–Pontypridd line, following Ty Mawr Road as far as Melingriffith water pump (GR 142799), which is in a fenced compound on the left.

This section of the trail passes through Hailey Park, another of Cardiff's many green areas. The Glamorganshire Canal ran on the east side of the park, and the sharp right- and left-hand turn leading to Old Radyr Road takes the trail back on to its course. The bridge under the railway at GR 145796 used to be a canal bridge, and much of Ty Mawr Road beyond has been built on the canal bed.

Melingriffith water pump is a very tangible reminder of the canal's existence. The Harfords of Melingriffith ran a tin-plate works here and were major investors in, and users of, the canal. However, they were badly affected by water shortages at this end of the navigation and frequently complained to the canal committee. In 1806 the engineer, John Rennie, was asked to report on water supplies, and it seems that

Melingriffith water pump was installed shortly afterwards as a result of his recommendations. The idea was to pump back into the canal water which had passed through the tin-plate works. The fact that this fragile-looking structure survived is little short of miraculous; after years of neglect it was restored to working order in 1980.

Melingriffith water pump is a useful landmark, for at this point the trail turns left and then right to rejoin the east bank of the Taff at GR 142800. It then follows the river round to the left, picking up the course of the Melingriffith Tramway at GR 143803. The course of the tramway is occupied by Forest Farm Road for a short distance, but at GR 138805 the two routes diverge: Forest Farm Road turns right, whereas the trail continues straight ahead. It then continues along the east bank of the Taff for a mile, passing under the M4 at GR 132815.

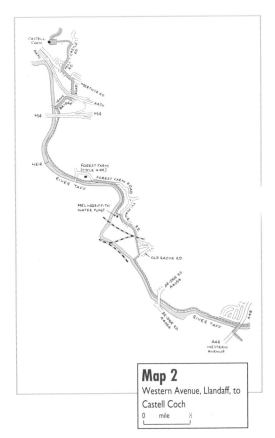

Map 2

Western Avenue, Llandaff, to Castell Coch

0   mile   ½

Apart from the canal and water pump, Melingriffith works was also served by a water-feeder from the Taff and a private tramway to quarries east of Pentyrch, which supplied iron ore. The tramway was built in about 1815 and later upgraded to a light railway, continuing in use until about 1959. It was approximately 2 miles long, running from GR 143803 to 128820. Its most notable feature was a rail-over-rail level crossing at GR 129818, where it ran diagonally across the four running lines of the Taff Vale Railway's busy route to Pontypridd – an arrangement guaranteed to cause operating problems for TVR staff. British Railways dismantled the crossing in 1962 and there can be little doubt that it was glad to see the back of it!

Forest Farmhouse (GR 137806) is an eighteenth-century Grade II listed building which is being restored by the British Trust for Conservation Volunteers as their regional headquarters. It is also the home of the Taff Trail Cycle Hire Centre, which is operated by Cardiff City Council in association with Merthyr & Cynon Groundwork Trust (see Appendix A for further details). Nearby, a mile-long stretch of the Glamorganshire Canal has been turned into a nature reserve, thanks to a successful campaign by the Cardiff Naturalists' Society in the 1960s. Approximately a hundred species of birds have been recorded here, including dippers and kingfishers which are extremely rare in other parts of Cardiff. The canal itself has been colonized by yellow water lily, which can be seen in flower throughout June. Those with an interest in the history of the site will be pleased to find a restored lock at GR 137809, the only one of the canal's fifty-one locks to survive.

A hundred yards after passing under the motorway, the trail turns right on to Iron Bridge Road, which it follows as far as Merthyr Road, Tongwynlais, at GR 134820. (Iron Bridge Road negotiates a right- and left-hand turn under the A470 at GR 134818: take care not to lose your way here.) On reaching Merthyr Road, turn left, pass the school and post office, then turn right into Mill Road. Follow this uphill as far as the main entrance to Castell Coch (GR 134827) and there turn left. It is a stiff climb to the castle, so you might welcome a visit as a chance to get your breath back. The next leg of the trail to Pontypridd starts from the right-hand side of the castle car park.

Iron Bridge Road takes its name from the iron bridge on the Melingriffith Tramway which conveyed the line from the east to the west bank of the Taff (GR 131816). It now conveys a footpath to the village of Morganstown.

Tongwynlais, like Nantgarw further north, is a village that has seen many changes in the twentieth century. A hundred years ago the Glamorganshire Canal and various railway lines converged here to pass through the narrow Nantgarw Gap. Now only the Taff Vale line to Pontypridd survives, modern transport needs being fulfilled by the M4 and A470 which meet at a vast intersection just south of the village. The Lewis family supplied Tongwynlais with its most famous resident, Mrs Mary Ann Wyndham Lewis, who married Benjamin Disraeli in 1839. The Lewis Arms in Mill Road commemorates the family of her first husband, Col. Henry Lewis.

Castell Coch marks the end of this section of the Taff Trail and is an architectural feature which cannot be missed. Although it occupies the site of a genuine Norman stronghold, it is another product from the team that created Cardiff Castle – the 3rd Marquis of Bute and his architect, William Burges. Castell Coch was begun in 1875, by which time work at Cardiff was already well advanced. The smaller castle is decorated in similar style, with ornate mouldings,

The main entrance to Castell Coch, another medieval fantasy from the team that redesigned Cardiff Castle in the 1860s. Although built on the site of a Norman fortress, the present structure is pure Victorian whimsy (David James Photography (Sussex))

gilded statues and mock-medieval paintings. The octagonal Drawing Room has scenes from *Aesop's Fables* on the walls, birds on the ceiling and butterflies on the ribs of the roof vaults. There is even a mock dungeon, which BBC Television used to good effect in its production of *The Prisoner of Zenda* in 1984. When you have seen Castell Coch, you will understand why it has proved so popular with film-makers; no doubt their fees make a worthwhile contribution towards its maintenance costs.

This is the second castle on the Three Castles Cycle Route which, in time, will be extended to Caerphilly. There, another visual surprise awaits unsuspecting visitors, for Caerphilly Castle sports a ruined tower which remains upright despite 'out-leaning the famous Tower of Pisa'. It has been in this state since Cromwell's troops tried to blow it up during the Civil War (1642–48). Caerphilly Castle occupies a 30 acre site and, together with Windsor and Dover, is one of the three largest castles in Britain.

2

CASTELL COCH TO PONTYPRIDD

THE TAFF VALE

8 MILES
EASY
ORDNANCE
SURVEY MAPS
1:50,000 Landranger
Sheets 170 and 171
1:25,000 Pathfinder
Sheets 1129 and 1148

Introduction

The high hills around Castell Coch announce in no uncertain terms that the Taff Trail has left the coastal plain occupied by Cardiff. North of the castle the trail heads for Nantgarw Gap, following the course of various disused railways which once criss-crossed the area. At the beginning of the twentieth century, no fewer than six lines belonging to six separate railway companies converged on this narrow pass, at a time when the Glamorganshire Canal was still open to traffic as well. Nowadays, only the Taff Vale line from Cardiff to Pontypridd and beyond remains open.

Nantgarw was once an important location on the Glamorganshire Canal and acquired a brief fame for its pottery. It also had a productive and long-lived colliery which finally closed in 1986. It is the point on the trail where the disused trackbed of the Alexandra (Newport and South Wales) Docks and Railway Company is reached. This was a colourful little railway whose line ran high up the east side of the Taff Vale. While this distanced it somewhat from would-be passengers, it means that modern walkers and cyclists have a very rural passage through what, on the valley floor, is an urban and industrial landscape.

History

Between Castell Coch and Pontypridd, the Taff Trail is constructed almost exclusively on disused railways, so this section looks at each of them in turn.

(1) The Barry Railway

After leaving Castell Coch and the wooded slopes of Fforest-fawr, the trail uses the trackbed of the Barry Railway's former Rhymney branch. The Barry Railway has had a bad press from transport historians, with some seeing it as a parasite which spread its tentacles across South Wales merely to extract business and profit from other, better-established lines. This is rather an unkind view. The real problem appears to have been the reluctance of the Bute Trustees to improve facilities at Cardiff Docks, which impeded the ability of collieries to export their coal. The final straw occurred in 1882, when the Trustees decided to increase their already high charges to finance the construction of the new Roath Dock.

As a direct result, a group of Rhondda colliery owners and South Wales shipping magnates united to promote a bill for a new dock at Barry with a network of connecting railways. After some early setbacks, they obtained their Act in 1884, with the dock and railway opening five years later. In its first year of trading (1889–90), the Barry Railway carried 3 million tons of coal, which suggests that it was fulfilling a genuine need. That it achieved this level of business at a time of price-cutting by the Taff Vale Railway and rebates from the Bute Trustees is all the more remarkable.

Encouraged by its early success, the company set about expanding wherever it could. The Act for the Rhymney branch was passed in 1896, with the line opening for goods and mineral traffic on 1 August 1901. This is a late date in railway terms and the Barry paid the price for being one of the last operators on the scene: wherever it went, it found the best ground already occupied by its rivals. This forced it to undertake some extravagant engineering, with each mile of the Rhymney branch proceeding by tunnel, viaduct or hillside ledge towards its destination. The most impressive feature on the line was Walnut Tree viaduct, which used to overlook Castell Coch before it was removed for scrap. This towering piece of Victorian engineering was 1,548 ft long, 120 ft high and crossed the valley on seven lattice girder spans.

There were hardly any passenger trains over this route, which is not surprising when one considers that, at its peak, eighty to ninety loaded coal trains were booked over it every day. A short-lived summer-only passenger service was provided between 1924 and 1935, but summer excursion trains fared better. These used to run from the Rhymney Valley to Barry Island and were a regular feature from 1905 to 1964. Given the line's many viaducts and high position in the valleys, it must have been an interesting and impressive ride.

Regular freight services were withdrawn on 17 June 1963. Mineral traffic survived for another four and a half years until 18 December 1967.

(2) The Rhymney Railway

Only a very short section of the Rhymney Railway is used in the Taff Trail but it is not without interest, being part of the company's original line from Rhymney to Cardiff. Present-day travellers between these two stations may be surprised to learn that, from 1858 to 1871, their journey would have been via Nantgarw and Radyr.

The Rhymney Railway was originally authorized in 1854, a subsequent Act of 1855 permitting an extension from Hengoed to the Taff Vale Railway at Taff's

Well. This line, now part of the Taff Trail, opened to freight and passenger services in early 1858. Running powers over the TVR provided access to Cardiff, but relations between the two companies were difficult, with the result that traffic on the Rhymney line was slow to develop. In order to resolve this problem, the Rhymney Railway promoted an independent route to Cardiff, which involved tunnelling beneath Caerphilly Common to reach the city from the north. This line was expensive to construct but finally opened to traffic on 1 April 1871.

One must assume that the opening of the direct line led to withdrawal of passenger services over the earlier route via Nantgarw; historical sources are strangely mute on the subject. In any event, freight services survived until very recently, for the line is shown as an operational 'Mineral Railway' on Ordnance Survey maps dated as late as 1989. It is likely that it conveyed coal traffic from collieries up the Bargoed Valley but closed with the decline of the Welsh coal industry.

(3) The Alexandra (Newport and South Wales) Docks and Railway

Despite the big name, this was a little railway whose main purpose in life was to act as a feeder for Newport Docks. While it was a prudent concern, it was run on a shoestring and became a repository for all sorts of second-hand locomotives and rolling stock. Its most remarkable vehicles were three American-style passenger saloons from the Barnum and Bailey circus train in which Buffalo Bill Cody toured the country in the early years of this century. These coaches must have looked an extraordinary sight as they trundled through the Taff Vale behind a clanking, second-hand saddle tank locomotive.

The story begins in 1865, when the Alexandra (Newport) Dock Company was incorporated to construct the North Dock at Newport. Despite delays and problems caused by the financial collapse of 1866, the dock duly opened in 1875, whereupon the company began to consider how it could bring itself more business. Judging that existing railways had already carved up trade in the valleys radiating from Newport, the company wisely decided to tap the coal traffic of the Taff and Rhondda valleys instead. It is tempting to think that companies like the Taff Vale Railway would have resisted such an approach, but it has to be remembered that the TVR and many of its local rivals were deeply dissatisfied with the facilities available at Cardiff Docks; the provision of rail access to rival docks at Newport was seen as a powerful bargaining chip.

Thus it was that the Pontypridd, Caerphilly and Newport Railway was launched in 1878. Although nominally independent, it was very much a satellite of the Alexandra Dock Company, the ultimate intention being to create a through route from Pontypridd to Newport. Such a route was opened in stages in 1884, 1886 and 1891, all achieved with the minimum of new construction. The first section to open was the PCN line from Pontypridd to Penrhos Junction (east of Nantgarw), the inaugural coal train running on 7 July 1884. The path of this train to Newport depended heavily on running powers over other companies' lines, but the Great Western Railway would have nothing of it: its signalman at Bassaleg Junction literally stopped the train in its tracks. It took over a fortnight of negotiations before the GWR acceded to PCN trains running over its metals, and regular services did not commence until 25 July 1884.

Being a late arrival in the Taff Vale, the PCN had to take a fairly high course along the east side of the valley, but this did not bother it particularly as it needed to gain height to reach the Rhymney Railway at Penrhos Junction. It mattered even less that this route was remote from the communities on the valley floor, for the PCN was conceived largely, if not entirely, as a coal-carrying railway. Given that the company saw little prospect of local passenger traffic, its first passenger trains were expresses which ran from the TVR station at Pontypridd to the GWR station at Newport; the only intermediate stop was at Caerphilly on the Rhymney Railway. This service operated from 28 December 1887 to 31 December 1916, when it was withdrawn as an economy measure.

In 1897 the PCN was absorbed by the Alexandra Dock Company, which had now renamed itself the Alexandra (Newport and South Wales) Docks and Railway Company; the grand name reflected the variety and geographical spread of its trading activities. In April 1904 the Alexandra began operating its own local passenger services from Pontypridd to Caerphilly, but in order to avoid paying junction tolls to the TVR at Pontypridd, it ran these from a new halt on the east side of the River Taff. This was called Pontypridd Tram Road Halt, which spoke volumes about the new service. All the intermediate stations – and there were many of them – were economical in the extreme. Access was by means of a gateway in the boundary fence, while a sprinkling of cinders at rail level served as a platform. At night the wooden nameboard was illuminated by a solitary oil lamp. When the Pontypridd–Newport expresses were withdrawn at the end of 1916, these rustic trains were extended from Caerphilly to Machen, where passengers were expected to connect with Newport services on the Brecon and Merthyr Railway (see Chapter 4).

A brief survey of the rolling stock and locomotives on the Pontypridd–Caerphilly line reveals just how eccentric these trains must have been. In 1904 and 1905 the company acquired two steam-powered 'railmotors' from Dugald Drummond's Govan Engineering Company. While these were fine when running on their own, they had insufficient power to haul extra carriages at busy periods. As a result, the company decided to use a locomotive and coaches for its passenger trains and converted the railmotors into ordinary carriages. The American-style saloons from Buffalo Bill Cody's circus train have already been mentioned: these were acquired in 1909, together with no less than twenty flat wagons originally used for transporting the circus's cages and road vehicles. Like the railmotors, these saloons were equipped with fixed steps for the benefit of passengers using the rail-level halts.

On the locomotive side, many of the company's engines were second-hand and some of them turned out to be real bargains, particularly those acquired from the Mersey Railway as a result of its electrification scheme. However, a pair of 1661 class 0–6–0 saddle tanks from the GWR were a different story: these turned out to have undersized coal bunkers, and brakes that were far from adequate when it came to stopping a heavy coal train on a descending bank! As a result, they sometimes appeared on passenger services, the 'standard' Pontypridd–Caerphilly train comprising a tank engine of dubious pedigree, a converted railmotor and one of the American saloons. The sight of one of these trains must have been unique, not just in South Wales but anywhere in the United Kingdom.

Space does not permit a more detailed study of this unusual railway, but its history contains much to surprise and amuse. It became part of the Great Western Railway on 28 March 1922, when the larger company re-acquired its unwanted 1661 class saddle tanks – a case of the biter bit. Passenger services between Pontypridd and Caerphilly survived until 17 September 1956, with freight services continuing until 31 July 1967. Prior to its re-use in the Taff Trail, the trackbed survived remarkably intact, with only a road and a river bridge at the northern end being removed.

Route Description

The trail to Pontypridd starts from the car park at Castell Coch with a mighty climb up the wooded slopes of Fforest-fawr. Most cyclists will be reduced to wheeling their machines up this bank, but there is a viewing platform halfway up which provides an opportunity to admire the views – and get one's breath back! At GR 132828 the trail turns sharp left: the turning is clearly waymarked and from here on cyclists can enjoy an effortless downhill ride as far as the Barry Railway at Ty Rhiw.

Fforest-fawr is owned by Forest Enterprise (formerly the Forestry Commission). Although it contains the usual conifer plantations, the Taff Trail passes through areas of mixed and deciduous woodland, including the mature beechwoods around Castell Coch and its grounds. It is surprising to discover that the northern part of the forest was used during the First World War as a training ground for tank drivers. Elsewhere, the remains of old iron workings and lime pits can be found, often no more than mounds or hollows in the ground.

At the edge of Fforest-fawr (GR 129836), the trail switches to the course of the Barry Railway, which it follows for a mile to GR 122849. It then turns left and runs downhill to the track of the adjoining Rhymney Railway, which it follows as far as the A468 at Nantgarw.

The trail leaves the railway at GR 126855 and runs up a short slope to the main road, which it negotiates by means of a pelican crossing. On the other side, turn left then right and second right into Heol-y-gors: follow this to the end at GR 127857, where a sharp left-hand turn leads onto the trackbed of the old Alexandra Docks line from Penrhos Junction to Pontypridd. This forms the next section of the trail to Pontypridd. Northbound cyclists will find that a gentle downhill gradient makes the going very easy.

The climb through Fforest-fawr is the only really steep section on the whole of the Taff Trail. On reaching the gentle gradients of the Barry Railway, one is inclined to wonder if it could not have provided an easier route from Castell Coch, but the answer is no: although the line skirts the western edge of Fforest-fawr, its course disappears into midair at the start of the now-demolished Walnut Tree viaduct.

The village of Ty Rhiw has a mixed ancestry. On the one hand, Ty Rhiw Farm is a relic from the pre-industrial age of scattered rural settlements, but the older terraced houses were built to accommodate miners working at nearby Nantgarw and Rockwood collieries. The first two shafts at Nantgarw colliery were started in 1910, being completed five years later when they had reached the then unprecedented depth of 856 ft. The mine continued in production until 1927, when

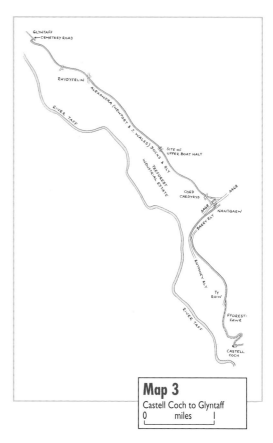

Map 3
Castell Coch to Glyntaff
0   miles   1

This imposing bridge once carried the Barry Railway over a mountain track at Ty Rhiw; now it is an access point to the Taff Trail. The mixed stone and brick construction is an unusual feature (author)

adverse geological conditions led to closure. It remained idle until 1946, when the Ministry of Fuel and Power approved plans to re-open it, and the following year, nationalization enabled the Nantgarw shafts to mine deposits other than those the colliery actually owned. These increased reserves kept the mine in production until 7 November 1986. Rockwood colliery, on the other hand, was a drift mine whose abandoned entrances lie on the hillside above Ty Rhiw; this was an earlier victim of contraction in the coal industry, having closed in the 1960s. (In a drift mine the shafts run horizontally, following the coal seam from the surface.)

The appearance of Nantgarw has been forcibly changed by modern road builders, who demolished numerous buildings in the 1970s to make way for the new A470; they left a road network on which speeding motorists hardly notice that the village exists. However, in the early nineteenth century Nantgarw was an important location on the Glamorganshire Canal. Many of the boatmen lived here, and they moored their boats close to their homes whenever possible. This created a certain amount of congestion, but it was nothing compared to the congestion caused by the treble locks just below the village, which had to be 'worked in turns'

Two walkers enjoy a stroll along the railway path between Nantgarw and Glyntaff. The railway followed a course high up the east side of the Taff Vale, well away from the industrial activity on the valley floor, which accounts for the rustic nature of this scene (Merthyr & Cynon Groundwork Trust/Hamish Park)

in order to conserve water. This involved working a single boat all the way up or all the way down, so that each lockful of water was used to pass two boats. Those waiting to travel north or south along the canal therefore had to wait for three locks to fill or empty.

Another unusual feature of Nantgarw was its pottery (GR 120854), which was founded by William Billingsley in 1813. It produced porcelain until 1822, when production difficulties forced it to close. Needless to say, any pieces of original 'Nantgarw ware' are now valuable collector's items. The story does not finish there, however, for the pottery was re-opened in 1833 to produce clay and earthenware tobacco pipes. This business sustained it until 1920, when the growing demand for cigarettes closed it for a second and final time. In recent years the site has been acquired by Taff Ely Borough Council, which plans to restore the overgrown 'Pottery House' and establish a small museum for the display and interpretation of the pottery's history and products. At the moment Glamorgan Gwent Archaeological Trust is conducting an archaeological investigation into the site, clearing, recording and stabilizing the overgrown factory buildings. Visitors can view the site and work in progress on payment of a small admission fee. (Opening hours: April to September, Wednesday to Sunday 10 a.m.–5 p.m. plus Bank Holiday Mondays.)

Between Nantgarw and Treforest, the Alexandra Docks and Railway line is now part of the Taff Trail. Its sylvan nature is revealed by the cascades of foliage hanging from this bridge at Upper Boat, once the site of a rail-level halt (author)

Having joined the trackbed of the Alexandra Docks line to Pontypridd, the noise and traffic of the busy A468 is quickly forgotten, for the old railway forms a delightful tree-lined avenue with some fine views over the valley to the left. In about a quarter of a mile it runs past Coed Caedyrys, a remnant of the oak woodland which once covered the valley sides. Another colliery used to be situated above the line on the right, and a tramway from this can be traced on the hillside running down towards the modern cycle track. Just beyond the wood the line offers a bird's-eye view of Treforest Industrial Estate on the left.

An abandoned pithead wheel alongside the former railway line from Penrhos Junction to Pontypridd reminds trail users how the wealth of the Taff Vale was won. The company which operated this line, the Alexandra (Newport and South Wales) Docks and Railway, had the longest title of any railway in the South Wales valleys (author)

Nantgarw colliery used to be situated at the southern end of this, its existence betrayed by the blackness of the ground.

At GR 114868 the line passes beneath a fine stone bridge which marks the site of Groeswen Halt. There was also a halt at Upper Boat at GR 107875. The name suggests a connection with the Glamorganshire Canal, which ran lower down the valley on the east side of the ill-fated Cardiff Railway or, more likely with the River Taff, which had a ferry crossing in the area. Both canal and railway are now buried beneath the new A470 dual carriageway, although a canal bridge survives in the vicinity at Pontmaes Mawr. The diminutive halt would have drawn many of its passengers from the tiny village of Pen-y-Groes, high up the slopes of Mynydd Meio. The presence of water beside the line reveals that the railway also had a drainage problem here, which local schoolchildren have helped to solve by creating a pond.

The next halt was at Dynea, the site of yet another colliery. This one was established in the early years of the nineteenth century, when Walter Coffin leased the land in this area for coal extraction. The output was shipped to Cardiff via the Glamorganshire Canal. The colliery occupied the hillside above the railway and its remains can be traced by walking down the footpath which starts at the Rose and Crown public house on Eglwysilan Road (GR 106889). The track passes through levels 3 and 4 of the old workings, with grassed-over spoil heaps and the remains of some old stone buildings in evidence.

By the time the railway arrives at Rhydyfelin, the Pontypridd conurbation has been reached. The off-road section of the trail comes to an end a mile later at

Glyntaff, where the railway company had a small engine shed. This was originally used for its two railmotors, but became the home of the passenger engines when the railmotors were converted into ordinary coaches. The railway path finishes by Glyntaff Crematorium, which is a reminder that the practice of cremation has its origins in Pontypridd. In 1884 a self-proclaimed Druid, Dr William Price, cremated the body of his infant son Iesu; the incident led to a famous court case at Glamorgan Assizes, which established the legality of cremation. Dr Price was a larger than life character who wore long hair, colourful clothing and a cap made from a whole fox's skin. He was also responsible for erecting the circle of stones on Pontypridd Common, which was used as a site for druidic rites.

The trail arrives in Glyntaff at Cemetery Road (GR 086892). Turn left here and continue straight ahead into Pentrebach Road, which is the A4054 to Abercynon. If you wish to avoid Pontypridd town centre, stay on the A4054 which becomes Merthyr Road. Follow this as far as GR 082909 on the north side of the town and there turn left into a minor road which curves left and then right, passing underneath the A470 dual carriageway. (These directions are continued in the next chapter.)

Alternatively, if you do wish to visit Pontypridd town centre, turn left at GR 080901 into Ynysangharad Road. Follow this to the roundabout at GR 076903 and proceed straight across, passing the entrance to Ynysangharad Park on your left. (This roundabout is extremely busy, so take great care when negotiating it.) Continue into Bridge Street, passing the Llanover Arms on your right. Cross the river to reach the traffic lights by the Historical and Cultural Centre and turn left. The town centre now lies ahead.

If you follow the waymarking down Ynysangharad Road, you will pass the Bunch of Grapes public house on the left-hand side. Apart from being an excellent pub with a range of real ales and good-value food, this is a handy landmark for identifying the course of the Glamorganshire Canal: a quarter of a mile of the old waterway runs behind the pub and past the works of Brown-Lenox Ltd. This company now manufactures stone-crushing equipment, but in the nineteenth and early twentieth centuries was a world-famous chain works, supplying the anchors and chains for vessels such as the *Great Eastern*, *Lusitania* and *Queen Elizabeth II*. As a matter of interest, Dr William Price, mentioned already in connection with the legalization of cremation, was the works' surgeon. Apart from practising druidic rites, Dr Price also had a strong social conscience and was indirectly involved in the Chartist rising in Newport in 1839. It is impossible to read the history of Pontypridd without coming across frequent reference to his many activities, and one wonders what the directors of Brown-Lenox made of him!

The imposing edifice of Eglwys Bach Surgery in Derw Road, Pontypridd, must come as a surprise to new patients. As the architecture reveals, it started life as a chapel (David James Photography (Sussex))

Ynysangharad War Memorial Park was purchased by public subscription and opened in 1923. With its avenues of mature trees and colourful flower gardens, it is one of Pontypridd's treasures and a fitting home for the James Memorial, which commemorates the lives and work of Evan James (1800–78) and his son James James (1832–1902). A plaque recalls how they 'inspired a deep and tender love of their native land, united poetry to song, and gave to Wales her National Hymn, *Mae Hen Wlad Fy Nhadau*'. Evan wrote the words and James the music.

The rest of Pontypridd is something of a mixed bag. The first thing which will impress itself on trail users is the sheer volume of traffic, which comes as a shock after the quiet seclusion of the railway path from Nantgarw. The second is the awkward juxtaposition of ancient and modern architecture. For example, at the junction of Bridge Street and Berw Road, two old chapels have been restored, one as the renowned Historical and Cultural Centre, the other as a doctors' surgery. Unfortunately, they are both dwarfed by a multi-storey car park which adjoins the equally dismal modern police station. The blame appears to lie with the planning policies of the 1970s, but there is now a greater interest in conservation and the town's appearance should improve in years to come. New roads are proposed to ease the traffic congestion and pedestrianization has already started in the town centre.

Old Bridge is Pontypridd's most famous landmark, having been built in 1756 by William Edwards, a self-taught mason. Its steep hump was always a bit much for traffic, so a new three-arched bridge financed by public subscription was built alongside in 1857 (David James Photography (Sussex))

Beyond Ynysangharad Park, Bridge Street crosses the River Taff with the distinctive Old Bridge on the right. This famous landmark was constructed in 1756 by William Edwards, a self-taught local mason, who was contracted to erect and maintain a stone bridge to replace the earlier wooden structures, all of which had been swept away by frequent and violent floods. Edwards made several attempts at solving the problem. When his first effort, a three-arched bridge, was swept away like its timber predecessors, he decided that the only effective solution was to construct a bridge with a single arch that would stand safely above any flood waters. His first two attempts to achieve this solution also collapsed, largely due to weight problems, but he then lightened the structure by forming three 'voids' or holes through each abutment. The resultant bridge stands to this day and, for forty years after its completion, remained the longest single-span bridge in the country. However, its steep arch was always a bit much for vehicular traffic, with the result that the present bridge was constructed alongside in 1857.

The town's Historical and Cultural Centre is the former Tabernacle Chapel, built in 1861, refurbished in 1910 and made redundant in 1983. It still possesses the original pipe organ, which is sometimes used for recitals. After its closure as a place of worship, it was acquired and restored by Pontypridd Town Council. It now contains a variety of exhibits, working models, recordings and archive films to illustrate the history of the area. There is a small admission charge, but it is well worth it if a journey along the Taff Trail has aroused your curiosity about the landscape and communities through which it passes.

Perhaps the most popular and colourful aspect of Pontypridd is its market. The present indoor market was built in the late 1870s, following the incorporation of the Pontypridd Market Company, which financed the venture with £30,000 raised from local subscribers. This seemingly modest sum represents about £4 million in today's money! Despite the economic decline experienced in the valleys during the 1920s and '30s, the market has always held its own and the Market Company is proud to have resisted wholesale redevelopment in favour of a gradual upgrading of existing buildings. Since 1985 the market area has become an important heritage site, with Market Street and Church Street being repaved in traditional materials and shop fronts being remodelled in sympathetic style. The end result combines an attractive and useful civic amenity in a largely genuine Victorian environment.

3

PONTYPRIDD TO MERTHYR TYDFIL

13 MILES
EASY
ORDNANCE
SURVEY MAPS
1:50,000 Landranger
Sheets 160, 170 and 171
1:25,000 Pathfinder
Sheets 1109 and 1129

THE GLAMORGANSHIRE CANAL

On this section of the trail, it is worth obtaining the two large-scale Pathfinder maps. The route is situated at the very centre of these sheets, whereas on the Landranger maps it is situated at the edge, which makes for some difficult juggling if you are trying to identify sites from six-figure grid references.

Introduction

North of Pontypridd the Taff Vale narrows considerably. Beyond Abercynon the urban and industrial development which has accompanied the trail all the way from Cardiff finally peters out. There is still plenty of ribbon development along the old main road, the A4054, but a short walk uphill from the valley floor quickly leads to extensive woodland or rugged mountain sides.

Abercynon was once an important trade centre, being the southern terminus of the Pennydarren Tramroad and the junction of the Aberdare and Glamorganshire canals. A fair amount of industrial archaeology remains here, the most notable example being the former aqueduct at GR 084949. This used to carry the Glamorganshire Canal from the west to the east side of the valley: nowadays it has been converted into a road bridge with the aid of a steel girder widening attached to its north elevation. North of Abercynon, the modern age becomes less intrusive: the A470 dual carriageway has destroyed part of the Glamorganshire Canal, but an interesting section of the Pennydarren Tramroad survives, and the canal itself materializes near Merthyr Vale to provide a level route for the last 5 miles into Merthyr Tydfil.

This famous iron town is the midpoint of the Taff Trail. It is a lot less awesome now than it was in the mid-nineteenth century, when it was never dark due to the raging furnaces which illuminated the night sky. The iron industry created great profit for the few and squalor for the many, so it is not surprising to learn that Merthyr produced a large number of radical politicians and Chartists, culminating in 1900 in the election of Keir Hardie as Britain's first Labour Party MP. Merthyr was renowned for the production of high-quality rails and its products were exported throughout the world from Russia to the United States. Its history is probably the most extraordinary and dramatic of any town in the United Kingdom.

History

There can be little doubt that the Glamorganshire Canal was the greatest and most prosperous of the South Wales canals. It was notable both in terms of engineering and profitability. On the engineering side, it fell 543 ft by fifty locks in its 25^1/$_2$ miles, the largest descent of any of the South Wales canals. On the profitability side, it suffered an embarrassment of riches and, at its height, was charging tolls that were massively below parliamentary levels. It was the trade route on which the prosperity of Cardiff and the Taff Vale was founded, and it is unfortunate that so little has survived to remind us of its importance.

The canal was promoted by the ironmasters of Merthyr, who wanted better transport for their finished goods. Although local roads had been improved by a number of turnpike trusts, a single road wagon could still convey only 2 tons of iron – far less than a fully loaded canal barge – and this made road transport uneconomical. Thus it was that an Act for the canal was obtained in 1790, authorizing a line from Merthyr to Cardiff via Pontypridd and Melingriffith. The company was authorized to raise capital up to £90,000 but, unusually, its dividend was limited to 8 per cent. The reasons for this are not entirely clear, but it seems that many of the promoters intended to use the canal themselves and wanted low tolls in preference to high dividends. If this is the case, they certainly got what they wanted. The major shareholder was Richard Crawshay of Cyfarthfa, who subscribed £9,600, with members of his family investing a further £3,500.

Construction began at the Merthyr end in August 1790, and by the spring of 1792 the canal was navigable from Merthyr to Pontypridd. It was opened throughout on 10 February 1794, with Richard Griffiths of Cardiff – a member of the committee – giving an 'entertainment in celebration', to which the company subscribed £14 11s 9d (£14.59). By now the canal included a half-mile extension at the northern end from Merthyr to Cyfarthfa, built to serve the Crawshay ironworks. An Act of 1796 authorized a further extension at the Cardiff end, which lengthened the canal by a mile to a sea lock on the River Taff. The Cardiff extension opened in June 1798, with the canal then attaining its full length of 25^1/$_2$ miles. Within a few years a large number of 'railways' had sprung up along its course, linking local mines with canal wharves where coal and other minerals were transshipped into barges.

In 1798 a serious and lasting feud erupted between Richard Crawshay and the other ironmasters who had invested in the canal. The nub of the argument was that Crawshay was using his influence as the major shareholder to run the canal for his own benefit, and there is evidence to demonstrate that he put pressure on boat owners to carry for Cyfarthfa rather than other ironworks. The outcome of this was that the owners of the Dowlais, Pennydarren and Plymouth ironworks were removed from the canal committee, whereupon they formulated plans for a rival tramroad which was to run from Cardiff to Quaker's Yard, with branches to serve important towns such as Merthyr Tydfil and Aberdare. The months that followed were characterized by much wrangling between the two groups, with demands, concessions and counterdemands passing to and fro. The canal company outplayed its rivals to the extent that a bill for the tramroad was withdrawn in May 1799, but the promoters went ahead and constructed the line without parliamentary authority.

What finally appeared was fairly modest in extent, being a 9½ mile line of 4 ft 2 in gauge from a junction with the Dowlais Tramroad (east of Merthyr) to the canal basin east of the aqueduct at Abercynon. The route, generally known as the Pennydarren Tramroad, was opened throughout in 1802 and, two years later, carved a niche in history by playing host to the first successful run of a steam locomotive on rails. The engine was designed by the Cornish engineer Richard Trevithick, and built almost entirely at Pennydarren ironworks. Rival magnates wagered as to whether it could complete a journey from Merthyr to Abercynon hauling a 10 ton load of iron. On 21 February 1804 the engine duly set out, hauling 5 wagons, 10 tons of iron and 70 men for good measure. Trevithick later wrote to a friend that the journey was '9 miles which we performed in 4 hours 5 minutes, but we had to cut down some trees and remove some large rocks out of the road. The engine, while working, went nearly 5 miles per hour.' He could have added that the locomotive broke a large number of the cast-iron rails; that its chimney stack had to be dismantled for it to pass through a tunnel; and that the track in the tunnel had to be re-aligned for the engine to get the full benefit of the arch. On top of all this, it had to be hauled back to Merthyr by horses because it could not manage the gradient. However, Trevithick had proved an important point which others, such as the Stephensons, were to exploit later in the century.

After this dramatic start, the Pennydarren Tramroad settled down to a generally uneventful life, although a major disaster occurred on 15 February 1815 when a timber bridge at Edwardsville collapsed with a train on it. This was replaced by a new stone structure, as was the bridge at the line's other river crossing at Quaker's Yard. After successful experiments, steam locomotives were introduced in 1833, by which time the tramroad was keeping to a regular timetable and even had fare-paying passengers. The cost of the round trip was 9d (4p), which entitled people to sit in, or on, a truckload of iron bars!

As for the tramroad's effect on the canal, there was practically none: there was so much trade in the Taff Valley at this time that both canal and tramroad could exist – and prosper – side by side. The tramroad was well used into the 1850s, but declined when the ironworks that had created it either switched their output to railways or closed. The final blow came in 1880 when the Plymouth works gave up making iron. After this the tramroad was converted into a railway between Merthyr and Mount Pleasant (south of Aberfan) and the rest abandoned.

Despite competition from the tramroad, the canal was seized upon as a means of communication and rapidly recouped its costs. By 1806 surplus funds were becoming a regular embarrassment: the size of the company's dividends was limited by Act of Parliament, so it resorted to successive toll reductions and regularly returned up to 20 per cent of toll income to traders. In 1816 and 1817 it even waived tolls completely for the last quarter of the year. These reductions led some contemporaries to call it the cheapest canal in the world, but they merely encouraged trade and produced yet greater surpluses. By 1833 the company's tolls were 85 per cent below parliamentary levels, and in December of that year it had to take steps to open the canal twenty-four hours a day. Double shifts of lock-keepers were appointed, and lighting was provided for both the tunnel at Cardiff and all locks.

From this it will be clear that the canal was operating at full capacity, and there were tremendous delays both at the sea lock and Nantgarw, where boats had to be worked individually through treble locks in order to conserve water. Ultimately, the problem at the sea lock was solved by the construction of Cardiff Docks, while the problem on the canal was solved by the construction of railways. Richard J. Hill of Plymouth works was one of the first to turn his mind to railways; I.K. Brunel was a friend of the Hill family and was invited to make his first survey in late summer 1835. The result was the Act for the Taff Vale Railway, which was passed in 1836. Like the canal before it, the TVR rapidly became the most prosperous railway in Britain, but it did not eclipse the canal as quickly as many had expected. By now coal was beginning to supplement iron as a cargo and this sustained canal traffic well into the 1860s; but then competition from local railways – and the new rail-connected docks at Cardiff – really began to bite.

The canal company proposed unsuccessfully to establish its own dock at Cardiff in 1865, 1866 and 1878. On the last occasion a bill for this was thrown out of Parliament as a result of effective opposition from Lord Bute, who had been behind – and profited immensely from – the development of Cardiff Docks generally. After this rebuff the canal was a spent force and Bute bought it outright on 19 November 1883. His motives are not entirely clear, but it is likely that he wanted to stop the company ever obtaining a dock to rival his own. Under the circumstances the terms of the purchase were generous, as were the improvements which soon followed at the southern end of the canal. However, Bute soon realized that he was throwing good money after bad; by 1888 the canal was carrying only minimal traffic and many were describing it as obsolete.

The rest of the canal's history is a sad tale of irreversible decline. In 1888 Lord Bute decided to promote a bill to turn the canal into a railway but nothing came of it; in 1893 steamboats were introduced but made no impact due to the large number of locks; and in 1897, traffic north of Pontypridd totalled a little over 30,000 tons in a whole year – barely 5 per cent of the levels forty years earlier. On 7 December 1898 the section from Merthyr to Abercynon was closed to all traffic. It remained derelict and unused until 1920, when Cardiff Corporation bought it as the course for a water pipe.

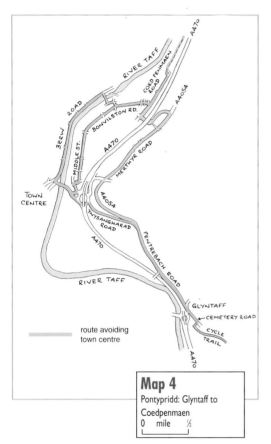

Map 4
Pontypridd: Glyntaff to Coedpenmaen
0   mile   ½

After 1898 the main value of the canal was as a water feeder, but a burst at Cilfynydd in 1915 precipitated closure of the Abercynon–Pontypridd section. A further burst at Nantgarw, on 25 May 1942, closed the Pontypridd–Cardiff section, after which only part of the sea-lock pound remained in use. Not surprisingly, 1942 was also the year in which the last boat passed along the cut. Cardiff Corporation bought the canal in 1943 and obtained an Act for its abandonment in the same year, although this stipulated that it should be kept open until six months after the end of the Second World War. How the Corporation could have met this requirement is difficult to see, unless it referred only to the short section south of Cardiff.

Route Description

The course of the Taff Trail through Pontypridd is complicated, but it is well signposted. In order to simplify the directions, they have been divided into sections which should be used as follows:

Route	Read sections
Northbound avoiding town centre	(1) and (4)
Northbound from town centre	(2) and (4)
Southbound to town centre	(3) only

(1) Route avoiding Pontypridd centre

If you have decided to miss the town centre, stay on the east side of the A470. Having proceeded out of Cemetery Road on to Pentrebach Road, you are on the A4054. Stay on this road, which becomes Merthyr Road, until you reach GR 082909 (see below).

If you have followed the signs down Ynysangharad Road to the roundabout at GR 076903, you have reached the busiest road junction in the town: this is situated beneath a large flyover on the A470, so you cannot miss it. Cycle around the roundabout and take the last exit before Ynysangharad Road, or if you are walking, turn right into it and go up the short, steep, Cornstores Hill. (Cyclists are advised to dismount at this roundabout and follow the directions for walkers.) Pass Llanover Road on the left, turn left into Merthyr Road at the top of the hill (GR 078904) and then continue north for half a mile.

On reaching GR 082909, turn left into a road which runs downhill and under the A470. This is signposted to Trallwng and leads to a T-junction with Coedpenmaen Road, where you should turn right. You are then back on the main course of the trail.

(2) Route from town centre northwards to Coedpenmaen Road

If you have followed the trail into the centre of Pontypridd, you can pick up the waymarking near the Old Bridge (GR 074904). Aim for the roundabout beneath the A470 but, just before reaching it, turn left into West Street, right into South Street, then left again into Middle Street. Follow Middle Street to a crossroads with Ralph Street, then continue straight ahead into Bonvilston Road. These are one-way streets, so take care not to turn off onto the southbound route where it crosses Bonvilston Road. Follow Bonvilston Road to the T-junction with Coedpenmaen Road. Finally, turn left and follow route description (4) to continue northwards along the Trail.

(3) Route from Coedpenmaen Road southwards to town centre

Due to the one-way traffic system, cyclists will find that this is different from the northbound route. Turn right off Coedpenmaen Road into Bonvilston Road and immediately

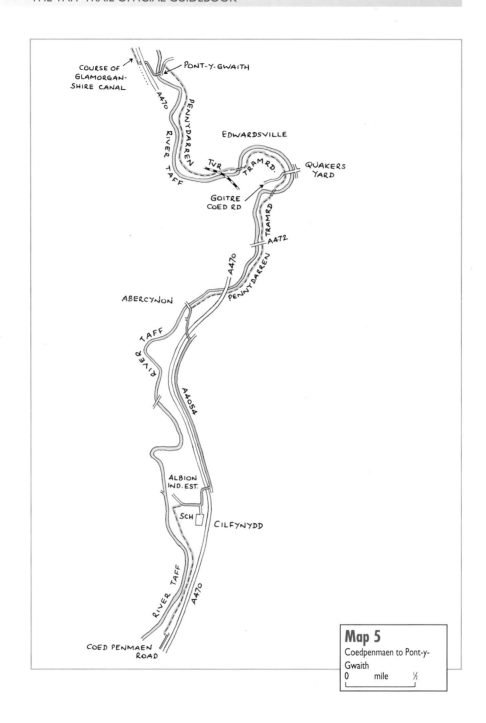

COURSE OF
GLAMORGAN-
SHIRE CANAL

PONT-Y-GWAITH

A470

PENNYDARREN

RIVER TAFF

EDWARDSVILLE

TVR

TRAM RD.

QUAKERS
YARD

GOITRE
COED RD.

TRAM RD

A472

A470

PENNYDARREN

ABERCYNON

RIVER TAFF

A4054

ALBION
IND. EST.

SCH

CILFYNYDD

RIVER TAFF

A470

COED PENMAEN
ROAD

Map 5
Coedpenmaen to Pont-y-
Gwaith
0   mile   ½

left into Thurston Road. Then take the first right into Crossways Street, following the signs across the northbound route to reach White Bridge at GR 077910 (note the fine view of the old Taff Vale Railway bridge upstream). Turn left into Berw Road, which follows the west bank of the Taff to the Historical and Cultural Centre and the Old Bridge at GR 074904.

(4) Route northwards from Coedpenmaen Road

Having reached Coedpenmaen Road, the going gets much quieter and easier. Follow the road to its end (GR 082912), then turn left on to a track which runs between the River Taff and the A470 dual carriageway. This swings right at GR 083927 and comes out on an unmade track which leads to Albion Industrial Estate (GR 086928), just north of Cilfynydd. Turn right here and follow the track until it becomes a metalled road. Pass the school entrance (also on your right), then turn left. Follow the road uphill and over the A470 to a T-junction with the A4054; now turn left towards Abercynon.

This elegant bridge at Trallwng used to carry the Taff Vale Railway's branch line from Pontypridd to Nelson. The line closed to passengers as long ago as 1932, but freight services survived over the southern section until 1949 (author)

This section of the trail utilizes a few scraps of the old TVR branch line from Pontypridd to Nelson. There were stations at Berw Road, Coedpenmaen and Cilfynydd, but the modern walker or cyclist will be hard pressed to find much evidence of them now. Most of the railway formation – and the Glamorganshire Canal which accompanied it – has been gobbled up by the new A470. The most tangible reminder of the line's existence is an elegant steel and stone bridge at GR 078911; trail users heading south will see this on their way through Trallwng. Cilfynydd achieved prominence in 1915 as the site of a breach in the canal bank and is also remembered for the Albion pit disaster.

The trail uses the A4054 for just over a mile to the edge of Abercynon. Happily for walkers and cyclists, the road turns out to be a fairly quiet route, with most of the traffic drawn away onto the nearby A470. At GR 084946, turn left at a set of traffic lights onto a road signposted to Abercynon. After crossing over the A470, turn right at another set of traffic lights and pass a church on the left-hand side. Just after this church, turn right into Tramroadside. (If you reach the bridge over the River Taff, formerly a canal aqueduct, you have gone too far.) This is the start of the course of the Pennydarren Tramroad which, with the Glamorganshire Canal, provides an easy route for most of the way to Merthyr Tydfil.

The Taff Trail bypasses Abercynon, whose steep streets and terraces lie on the other side of the river. Its importance in the nineteenth century is difficult to envisage today, but much of the town's activity centred on the aqueduct which is now the roadbridge at GR 084949. West of this, the Aberdare and Glamorganshire canals met at a junction, while to the east was a large basin which served as the southern terminus of the Pennydarren Tramroad. The Navigation public house used to be the headquarters of the canal company, while a plaque outside the nearby fire station commemorates Trevithick's famous locomotive run in February 1804. If you have time, a short section of the Glamorganshire Canal can be traced on the west side of the river at GR 086952: it survives as a grassy expanse by a lane behind a row of houses.

Victoria Bridge once carried the Pennydarren Tramroad from the north to the south bank of the River Taff at Quaker's Yard. The central span, originally timber, was rebuilt in stone in 1815 when its sister bridge at Edwardsville collapsed with a train on it (David James Photography (Sussex))

After the twists and turns between Pontypridd and Abercynon, it is a relief to get onto the direct route of the Pennydarren Tramroad. The engineer, George Overton, kept to the course of the Taff wherever possible and the river can often be seen or heard on the left-hand side. There are a number of dwellings alongside the track, especially near Quaker's Yard, many of which look as if they date from the line's construction. At the beginning of the nineteenth century, many roads were still in appalling condition and locals thought nothing of walking on, or alongside, the tramroad as a quicker means of getting from A to B. It was partly in an attempt to capitalize on this, and partly for reasons of public safety, that the Pennydarren and other tramroad companies began to carry passengers.

North of Quaker's Yard, the Taff Trail passes through a steep-sided wooded gorge, which is resplendent with colour in the autumn. This was part of the Pennydarren Tramway, traversed in 1804 by Trevithick's pioneering steam locomotive (Rhodri Clark, Cardiff Cycling Campaign)

Between Quaker's Yard and Edwardsville, the tramroad crosses the river twice, being forced to do so by the lack of space on its east side. Two substantial bridges, comprising a single span each, stand astride the river at GR 094963 and 090965. Both are now scheduled as ancient monuments, and both were constructed in 1815 to replace earlier timber structures. The timber bridge which collapsed was the northern one at Edwardsville: close inspection of its abutments will reveal the recesses where the timbers were once fitted.

The tramroad crosses Goitre Coed Road between these two bridges, at the site of a former level crossing (GR 096965). This is a convenient place to break your journey if you wish to visit Quaker's Yard; the village has two pubs and a convenient general store within yards of the trail. Its unusual name derives from the fact that there is a burial ground nearby for the Society of Friends. Nowadays Baptists are more in evidence than Quakers: they worship at Berthlwyd Chapel, off Wingfield Terrace. This is a finely maintained building in the classical style dating from 1880, erected to replace an earlier chapel of 1649.

There is more industrial archaeology back on the trail, for after the tramroad's second crossing of the river, the track passes beneath Quaker's Yard viaduct on the TVR line from Pontypridd to Merthyr. This was opened in 1841 but widened in 1862, when the whole line was doubled to cope with increasing traffic; the join can still be seen: The viaduct remains in use for trains on BR's 'Valley Line', and in recent years has acquired Grade II Listed Building status. The tramroad then enters a delightful sylvan stretch where the stone-block sleepers which supported its primitive rails are still in place. These start at GR 084966 and continue northwards for about a mile.

At GR 080967 and again at GR 083968 will be seen the remains of two more viaducts. The first of these conveyed the Newport, Abergavenny and Hereford Railway into the Aberdare Valley via the 703 yd Cefn Glas tunnel, while the second carried a joint line of the Great Western and Rhymney railways onto the west bank of the Taff, which it then followed all the way to Merthyr. Dr Beeching closed the Newport, Abergavenny and Hereford line in 1964, but the joint line to Merthyr went ten years earlier. Before passing on, try to imagine what this place must have been like a hundred years ago: the disused tramroad on this side of the valley, the abandoned canal on the other, and trains passing alongside and overhead on three separate routes – all servants to the steady outpouring of iron, steel and coal.

At GR 080977 the Taff Trail swings sharply to the left and leaves the Pennydarren Tramroad behind. It then runs south alongside the river before negotiating a U-turn to the right which takes in the ancient Pont-y-Gwaith bridge (GR 080976). The trail then passes under the A470 by a short tunnel before joining the course of the Glamorganshire Canal at GR 079977. Turn right here and it is then straight on – more or less – all the way to Merthyr.

The link from the tramroad to the towpath of the canal is an important point on the Taff Trail, for there are four old bridges here within a quarter of a mile. The first of these is situated at GR 081978 and carries the parish road over the 1841 Taff Vale Railway line. The second adjoins it and is a magnificent stone bridge over the Pennydarren Tramroad, affording a good view of a passing loop on the line. Next comes Pont-y-Gwaith or 'bridge of the works', constructed some time between 1811 and 1828 to provide access to a local ironworks. This was seriously damaged in 1989, but the creation of the Taff Trail provided the impetus to restore it, the work being completed in mid-1993. Finally, the biggest surprise of all, is Pont-y-derwen (GR 079976), a stone bridge which crosses the empty bed of the Glamorganshire Canal. This is extremely rare, to say the least: the only other example of which the author is aware is the iron bridge from Rhydycar, which was moved upstream to a new site in Merthyr Tydfil (see next chapter).

The next mile is fairly uneventful, with the trail keeping close to the west side of the A470. Fortunately, the old canal retains a secluded atmosphere and is not much disturbed by traffic noise, although one wonders how it managed to escape destruction when the new road was built.

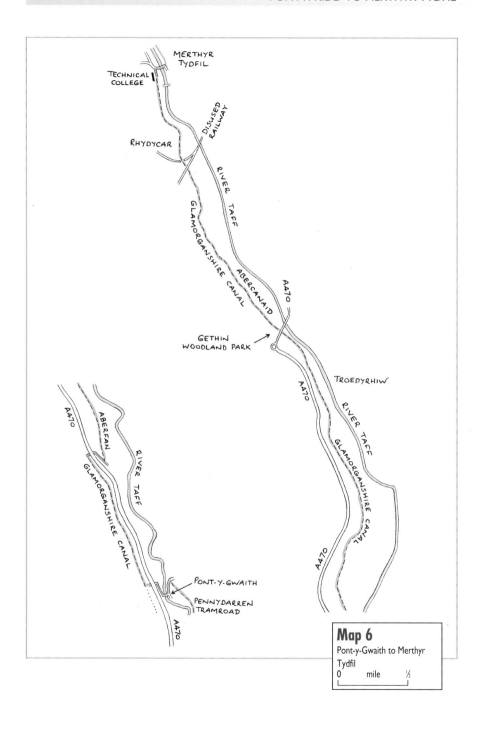

Map 6

Pont-y-Gwaith to Merthyr Tydfil

0 mile ½

> At GR 071992 the trail turns sharp right, passes under the A470, runs downhill for 200 yd and then turns sharp left. These dogleg turns mark the point where the A470 crosses the cut, but the towpath then resumes its northward course uninterrupted.

The trail has now entered the former mining village of Aberfan, which achieved tragic fame in 1966 when the local tips slipped, crushing many houses and the village school. Like many Welsh villages, Aberfan was well provided with nineteenth-century chapels, although some are now in disrepair. The Aberfan Inn in Aberfan Road is close to the trail and provides a convenient stop for refreshments.

On leaving Aberfan, the canal regains open country, accompanied by the Great Western and Rhymney railways' joint line from Quaker's Yard to Merthyr, which appears first on the right and then on the left. The industrial wealth of its terminus clearly attracted railways like bees to a honey pot.

The next settlement of any size is Troedyrhiw, most of which is situated on the opposite bank of the river. However, the parish church of St John the Baptist is located just off the canal towpath at the western edge of the village and has a rather colourful history. It was built in 1852 as a result of the generosity of the Hill family, owners of the Plymouth ironworks. The only person buried there is Anthony Hill (1785–1862), whose remains are apparently interred in a series of three coffins: 'An elm inner shell with white flannel lining and a pillow; a lead middle shell; then an outer shell of "heart of oak", with black nails, black trimmings and a black plate on the lid.' This extravagant casket is lodged beneath the communion table.

Pont-y-Gwaith, north of Edwardsville, literally means 'bridge of the works'. The information in published sources is conflicting, but it appears to have been constructed between 1811 and 1828 to provide access to a local ironworks. The architect is reputed to have been William Edwards, who built Old Bridge at Pontypridd (Merthyr & Cynon Groundwork Trust)

Viewed by today's standards, Anthony Hill seems slightly at odds with himself, for he was a noted local philanthropist yet an equally famous opponent of trade unions. When he died in 1862, the stained-glass window above the altar was installed, with each of his workers donating a day's pay towards the cost; at least they were given a day off for the funeral! His influence lives on, for Anthony Hill Scholarships have been available in recent years to descendants of his employees.

At the other end of the social scale, Troedyrhiw also possesses Furnace

Row, a terrace of canalside cottages at GR 065025. These were built in the 1860s for workers at the nearby Castle and Furnace pits. Although much altered, some of the units feature 'house over house' construction, with the upper dwellings facing the canal and the lower dwellings facing the street. The nearby Dynefor Arms dates from the late eighteenth century and was possibly built as a canalside pub. It is a friendly hostelry with some original features and makes another convenient refreshment stop along the way.

> **At GR 062032 the canal passes under the A470 for the last time. It continues through Abercanaid and Rhydycar before arriving in Merthyr by the technical college (GR 046061). Turn right onto Penry Street bridge then cross the road to follow the eastern bank of the River Taff for the continuation of the trail towards Brecon.**

The final crossing of the A470 is a convenient landmark for Gethin Woodland Park, which is situated just to the west of the trail at GR 061032. The park comprises an area of mixed woodland with a variety of facilities, including a car park, a children's play area, toilets and forest trails. The site of Gethin No. 1 Pit, once mined for its steam coal, is situated nearby on the east side of the towpath.

Abercanaid is another village of terraced streets laid out parallel to the lines of communication along the valley. Like Furnace Row at Troedyrhiw, Pond Row is a 'house over house' terrace built in the mid-nineteenth century from local rubble (recycling is not an entirely modern phenomenon!). One pair of houses has a rounded corner and window at canal level, apparently to keep an eye on canal traffic. Abercanaid also had its own magnate, in this case Sir William Thomas Lewis, Baron Merthyr of Senghenydd. Lewis started work at the Plymouth ironworks but progressed to become a coal baron, owning the Lewis Merthyr collieries in the Rhondda. He is commemorated by a statue in Upper Thomas Street, Merthyr. The Llwynyreos Inn, situated at the north end of the village, is another canalside pub that has survived into the modern age.

Glyndyrus locks (numbers 4 and 5 on the canal) were situated a mile south of Merthyr at GR 051046. While they have long been demolished, the adjoining lock cottage survives in private ownership. It was built between 1806 and 1808 at a cost of £60 and was used by boatmen as an overnight stopping place. They would store their barges in a low tunnel outside the cottage and sleep in a small building nearby. The tunnel still survives, its entrances betrayed by grilles near the towpath, half-hidden by undergrowth.

Beyond Glyndyrus locks the canal passes under two railway bridges in quick succession. The first, a triple-arched stone structure, once carried the Vale of Neath Railway from Merthyr to Neath; the second, now bereft of its steel span, used to carry the joint Brecon and Merthyr/LNWR line to Morlais Junction (see next

This triple-arched bridge at Rhydycar once carried the Vale of Neath Railway from Merthyr to Hirwaun (Gelli Tarw Junction) over the Glamorganshire Canal. The railway outlived the canal by sixty-four years, but now their roles are reversed: the canal towpath is busy with cyclists while the railway trackbed remains empty and unused (author)

chapter). Rhydycar Junction, once a busy spot on the local railway network, lies to the north-east at GR 051053, but Rhydycar is better known nowadays for its leisure centre.

Arrival in Merthyr comes as a mild surprise, for the Taff Trail enters the town by a route that avoids many of the usual preparations: there are no terraced houses, no signs, no advertising hoardings – and it is all the better for it. However, the scenery around the college is the result of a twentieth-century road-improvement scheme and would look just as much a part of Hemel Hempstead or High Wycombe. It certainly gives no indication of Merthyr's history.

The first blast furnace was built at Cyfarthfa ironworks in 1765 by Anthony Bacon. The works later passed into the hands of the Crawshay family, which by the 1820s had developed it into the largest and most advanced ironworks in the world. The demand for iron led to an unprecedented growth in the town's population: it was considered large in 1801 when it exceeded 8,000, but fifty years later it had reached 46,000, nearly half of whom were directly employed in the iron industry. As noted earlier, this explosion of trade created vast profits for the few and squalor for the many. Child labour was endemic, often because financial hardship forced parents to bring their children to work with them. Older children were employed at the blast furnaces to break up limestone, and, when coal mining developed, the younger ones went underground to operate fire doors or haul trams through tunnels less than 3 ft high. It was a volatile mixture, so it is not surprising that serious riots occurred in 1801, 1816 and 1831. These led to a military garrison being stationed permanently in the town – a case of treating the symptoms rather than the cause.

Nowadays the conditions that led to these riots are a faded memory, but the town's extraordinary history has created an unparalleled legacy of industrial archaeology. Examples of practically everything survive, from blast furnaces to engine houses, from

Trevithick's tunnel at Merthyr Tydfil, believed to be on the course of the Pennydarren Tramway, was restored in 1991 as part of the 150th anniversary celebrations of the Taff Vale Railway, which reached Merthyr in 1841. A mural has been constructed just within the portal, depicting Trevithick's historic steam locomotive run in 1804 (David James Photography (Sussex))

workmen's cottages to ironmasters' castles. As the next section of the trail passes directly by many of these features, they are described in the next chapter, but it is appropriate here to mention Trevithick's tunnel, which is situated at the southern end of the town near the Hoover factory (GR 056047). This was restored and opened in April 1991 as part of the 150th anniversary celebrations of the opening of the Taff Vale Railway line to Merthyr. It is believed to be on the course of the Pennydarren Tramroad, which would make it the tunnel where Trevithick had to remove his engine's chimney stack. Given that the tramroad passed on the east side of Merthyr to make a connection with the Dowlais Tramroad, it is in a highly probable location.

4

17 MILES
ENERGETI
ORDNANCE
SURVEY MAPS
1:50,000 Landranger
Sheets 160 and 161
1:25,000 Outdoor Leisu
Map II and Pathfinder
Sheet 1109

MERTHYR TYDFIL TO TALYBONT-ON-USK

THE BRECON & MERTHYR RAILWAY

Introduction

After the long climb from Cardiff, the trail finally leaves the Taff Valley and enters the Brecon Beacons National Park. The section from Merthyr to Cefn Coed is urban, but the trail then takes to the trackbed of the former Brecon & Merthyr Railway, which leads it through the valley of the Taf Fechan as far as Pontsticill. Here the dam of Pontsticill Reservoir is crossed before the trail begins a wooded ascent to Taf Fechan Forest. This is followed by the summit (1,450 ft), after which the Brecon & Merthyr Railway is regained for the 7 mile descent to Talybont-on-Usk – a real luxury for cyclists.

In years gone by, travellers on the Brecon & Merthyr noticed a dramatic change as their trains finally climbed out of the smoke-hung Taff Valley, for the mountain barrier north of Merthyr separated the industrial valleys from a rural idyll of rugged pastures and sheep farms. Nowadays the contrast is less dramatic (the decline of the iron and coal industries has seen to that), but it is still striking. In place of the large valley communities with their long ribbons of terraced cottages, we now find a world of isolated farms, narrow country lanes and rambling villages.

History

Despite its title, the Brecon & Merthyr Railway actually extended from Brecon to Bassaleg, 3 miles west of Newport. The link to Newport was absolutely vital, for this carried the lucrative industrial traffic which enabled the company to support the hopelessly uneconomic service over the mountains to Brecon. As it was, the cost of operating the line to Brecon kept the company in penury for nearly forty years and gave it an unenviable reputation. The Midland Railway derided it as '60 miles of single line unable to earn its keep' and, according to the railway historian Derek Barrie, the company's passenger services were for generations 'a popular byword for sloth and unpunctuality'. Bad reputations are not the prerogative of modern railways!

The story of the B&M began in 1856, when a group of local promoters appointed the London engineer, Henry Conybeare, to survey a route from Brecon to Merthyr. An optimistic prospectus followed in 1858, which promised better communications than offered by either the Brecknock and Abergavenny Canal (see next chapter) or the Brynoer Tramway. The usual benefits were suggested: agricultural produce from around Brecon could be taken to market in Merthyr and Dowlais more easily, while coal, iron and lime would be transported the other way, all at considerable savings to the local populace.

These arguments were enough to convince Parliament and the company duly received its Act on 1 August 1859. Developments during the next few years were extremely complex as the young company fought territorial and legal battles with its neighbours. Many of these centred on re-use of the old Hay Railway, a horse-drawn affair of 1811 which rival companies wanted to use as their eastern approach to Brecon.

While all this was going on, construction of the B&M was inaugurated on 18 January 1860 at separate ceremonies either side of Torpantau tunnel, then known as Beacon or Summit tunnel. Equipment and materials for construction were conveyed by the Brecknock and Abergavenny Canal and the Brynoer Tramway, but progress was painfully slow due to the 'unprecedented wetness' of the mountain weather. The two cuts at Torpantau tunnel were finally joined on 11 January 1862, and on 28 August that year a trial run was provided for the directors and their friends from Dowlais to Talyllyn, 4 miles east of Brecon.

By this time the B&M had obtained the necessary powers and legal agreements to take over the Hay Railway between Talyllyn and

This elaborate iron canopy used to cover a fountain, built in 1906 to commemorate Robert and Lucy Thomas, pioneers of the local coal trade. As can be seen, only the canopy now remains; it is situated outside St Tydfil's Church at the bottom of Merthyr Tydfil High Street (Merthyr & Cynon Groundwork Trust)

A close-up of one of the arches of Cefn Coed viaduct. This massive structure is 770 ft long, 115 ft high and crosses the valley of the Afon Taf Fawr in fifteen spans of 39 ft 6 in each. It is the third-largest viaduct in Wales (David James Photography (Sussex))

Brecon, but progress was again slower than expected because the Hay Railway was still in use; the regular passage of horse-drawn 'trains' naturally interrupted the reconstruction work. Nonetheless, the link was completed in 1863 and a single line from Brecon to Dowlais opened for passengers and goods on 23 April. The official opening followed on 1 May with the usual junketings and speeches. It is interesting to note that at this stage passengers for Merthyr had to alight at Pant and change to a horse-drawn bus, an arrangement which has echoes of weekend engineering works on the modern railway.

The company had obtained an Act for a branch line to Merthyr in 1862 and work on this progressed slowly until 1866. Henry Conybeare had attempted to survey a route for this line as long ago as 1857, but he worked along the east side of the Taf Fechan Valley and ended up in the grounds of Cyfarthfa Castle, whence he was forcibly ejected by no less a person than William Crawshay, the local iron magnate. With this unfortunate experience in mind, the company now selected a route down the west side of the valley, which guaranteed the support of the powerful Crawshay family but involved considerable engineering expense. The still-visible signs of this are the huge viaducts at Pontsarn and Cefn Coed, described in more detail below.

Life was never easy for the young Brecon and Merthyr Railway and, as if to prove the point, its banking house collapsed in 1866 with liabilities of £11 million – a colossal sum in those days. Unfortunately, this left the Merthyr branch incomplete, marooned in midair on the half-built Cefn Coed viaduct. The B&M went into receivership shortly afterwards and the next two years were very difficult as a financial restructuring was agreed with the company's creditors. It is to the receiver's credit that construction work on the Merthyr branch continued during this period, with services opening to Cefn Coed on 1 August 1867 and to Merthyr Tydfil High Street exactly a year later.

By this stage, the lines that are now used in the modern Taff Trail were complete, but one final development remained. In the early 1870s the B&M found itself in regular conflict with the mighty London and North Western Railway, which was pushing south and west into Wales via its Heads of the Valleys line from Abergavenny. (Ironically, parts of this route are now subsumed in improvements to the Heads of the Valleys road, the A465.) In 1874 the LNWR promoted a bill for its own line from Dowlais to Merthyr, which the B&M naturally opposed, fearing loss of revenue on its own route between these towns. Eventually an agreement was reached whereby the B&M withdrew its opposition to this bill in return for its Merthyr branch becoming joint with the LNWR. The LNWR also undertook to reimburse 50 per cent of the line's construction costs at £25,000 per mile, a persuasive factor given the B&M's still straitened financial circumstances.

Thus it was that on 1 January 1879, LNWR services began operating to Merthyr Tydfil via Morlais Junction, Pontsarn and Cefn Coed. Morlais Junction took its parts. This new connection must have cost the LNWR dear, for it had to tunnel beneath the existing B&M lines to Dowlais and Newport: the new line popped out of a sheer rock face about a mile east of Pontsarn viaduct.

By this time the B&M network was complete and the company settled down to nearly a quarter of a century of service to the local community. Its profits were never vast (the fearsome gradients on the line through Torpantau tunnel saw to that) but they were not hopeless either, especially after the turn of the century. In 1921, the last year of the company's independent existence, it carried approximately two and a half million passengers and four million tons of freight, and paid the full dividend of 4 per cent on both its first and second preference shares. This was not bad going in a year that was affected by a three-month-long national coal strike.

However, the Railways Act of 1921 had now been passed in an attempt to reconstruct the nation's railways after the First World War. Many companies had been run into the ground by the war effort and faced huge backlogs of maintenance and investment. The Act provided for the so-called 'grouping' of railways into four major companies, and the Brecon and Merthyr accordingly became part of the Great Western Railway on 1 July 1922.

Unfortunately for rail transport everywhere, the necessities of war had led to tremendous improvements in road transport, and bus services soon began to drain passengers from the trains. In South Wales this problem was exacerbated by the closure of many historic ironworks and a prolonged depression in the coal industry. The Second World War brought renewed activity to the line, but it was no more than an Indian summer: after 1945 decline set in again, with the inevitable closures in its wake. The passenger services were the first to go, being withdrawn between Pontsticill and Merthyr on 13 November 1961, and between Brecon and Dowlais on 31 December 1962. Freight services survived until 4 May 1964, but then they too were withdrawn except over a 4 mile section between Merthyr and Vaynor Quarry. The end for this last surviving stub of the old LNWR joint line came on 3 October 1966.

Route Description

Starting at Merthyr College, proceed to the main road and turn right to cross Penry Street bridge. Cross the road and follow the riverside path to the end of Dixon Street and a signalled crossing. Cross into Bethesda Street opposite and turn left at the T-junction into Quarry Row which leads to a riverside path.

This section of the Taff Trail passes by, or very close to, many of the historic sites of Merthyr Tydfil. The first of these is Ynysfach engine house (GR 045061), which is just behind the college; it is signposted on the left from Penry Street.

Anyone viewing the smartly restored exterior of this building today would be hard-pressed to imagine what it was like in its heyday. The engine house originally held a beam engine which blew air into the adjoining blast furnaces; these survive alongside and are soon to be restored as well. The furnaces were used to produce pig iron, an impure form of iron, which was transported to Cyfarthfa ironworks for refining. The pig iron was produced from coke, iron ore

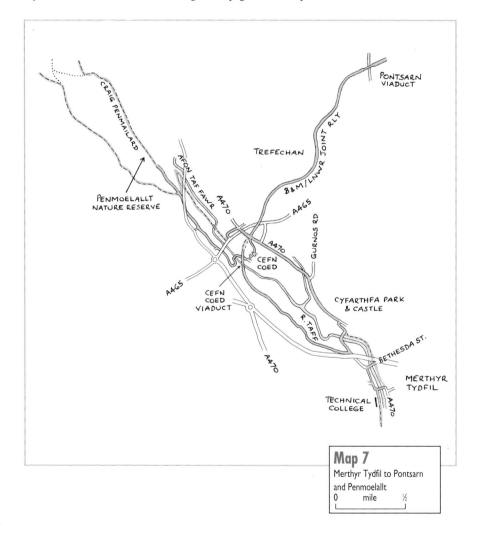

Map 7

Merthyr Tydfil to Pontsarn
and Penmoelallt

0   mile   ½

Ynysfach engine house was opened in 1801 to supply a constant flow of air to the blast furnaces situated to the left of this picture. It was rebuilt in 1836 and closed in 1874, when Robert Thompson Crawshay decided that closure was preferable to meeting union demands (David James Photography (Sussex))

and limestone, which were loaded into the furnaces from above; women were employed to break up the limestone at a rate of 12 tons a day. The purpose of the beam engine was to provide the constant flow of air necessary to keep the furnaces burning at a high temperature.

The present engine house was opened by Richard Crawshay in 1801 and, as far as can be judged from contemporary illustrations, was rebuilt in 1836. It is believed that Ynysfach was an experimental site, being the first of the Crawshay furnaces to use steam rather than water power for the blast. If this was the case, the experiment was highly successful, for Ynysfach produced about 40 per cent more pig iron per week than other furnaces in the area.

The Ynysfach engine worked regularly until 1874, when Robert Thompson Crawshay closed it rather than give in to what he regarded as the excessive demands of the unions. This was effectively the end of the engine's working life, for after 1879 a new generation of Crawshays switched production to steel. By the early 1980s Ynysfach engine house was just an empty shell, but a restoration programme began in 1986. This concluded in August 1990, when the Duchess of York opened the building in its present form. Internal floors have been added (originally, the beam engine occupied all the internal space) and these now accommodate an award-winning heritage centre which describes Merthyr's industrial history.

A short detour from the trail leads to the birthplace of Dr Joseph Parry, the composer. This may be reached by turning left and then immediately right at the end of Dynevor Street. No. 4 Chapel Row (GR 044066) is one of a terrace of cottages built in 1825 by the Cyfarthfa Iron Company for skilled workers at the nearby ironworks. Parry was born here, into relative poverty, on 21 May 1841. The subscriptions of Welsh men and women in his native country and America enabled him to enter the Royal Academy of Music, London, and then Cambridge University, where he obtained his music degree. His compositions include songs, hymns, operas, oratorios and cantatas, some of which are still in today's concert repertoire. Chapel Row was completely restored by Merthyr Tydfil Borough Council in 1978 and No. 4 is now open to the public. The ground floor has been refurnished as it might have looked in Parry's day, while an exhibition on his life and work has been assembled upstairs. Opposite, a short section of the Glamorganshire Canal has been excavated. This is spanned by an iron bridge which has been moved here from downstream at Rhydycar.

The remains of the nearby chapel of ease predate Chapel Row. During the 1850s this building was used as the rehearsal room for Cyfarthfa Brass Band, a reminder that Victorian chapel-goers saw music as a civilizing influence on the working classes.

Follow the riverside path to Williamstown, where the route emerges by a long row of terraced cottages. In the future, the trail will cross the road and enter Cyfartha Industrial Estate opposite. You will then cross the river via a new bridge to join the existing trail. In the interim, please follow the route described on p. 53.

William Crawshay II built Cyfarthfa Castle in 1825, choosing a vantage point high above Merthyr Tydfil from which he could survey his empire by day and night. It was purchased by Merthyr Corporation in 1909 and now accommodates a school, museum and art gallery (Merthyr & Cynon Groundwork Trust)

The artificial lake in front of Cyfarthfa Castle had been drained temporarily when this photograph was taken, but its scale can still be appreciated. The construction of Cyfarthfa Castle cost William Crawshay II some £30,000, but he had to pay nearly as much again to create a lake halfway up the hillside. Note Cefn Coed viaduct in the distance: the Crawshays may have evicted the Brecon and Merthyr Railway to the far side of the valley, but they still had to look at it (author)

The fact that Cyfarthfa Castle (GR 041073) is not a genuine defensive structure is revealed by its neatness and uniformity. It was built in 1825 as a grand family home by William Crawshay II, the third in the Crawshay dynasty, who wanted an imposing residence to overlook his nearby ironworks, which were then the largest in the world. The castle complex cost £30,000 to build and, apart from the seventy-two rooms, included a dairy, a brewery, a vinery and a pinery (a special glasshouse for growing pineapples). The castle is fronted by a large terrace which overlooks a man-made lake. This cost almost as much to build as the castle due to problems with making the bottom watertight, but its purpose was practical as well as decorative, for it formed a feeder pond for the ironworks in the valley below.

The castle was sold to Merthyr Corporation in 1909, which converted it into a museum and school. Both are still flourishing, the museum having been joined by an art gallery which houses an important collection of twentieth-century works. The castle also contains a commemorative Taff Trail brick relief, completed at the Trail launch ceremony in June 1993. The estate has recently secured grants of over £800,000 to invest in improvements, and this will see the former 'state rooms' restored to their 1830s splendour. Part of the money will also be spent on the surrounding grounds, which comprise 160 acres of rolling parkland and broad-leafed woodland. The trees here include several rare and exotic species, such as *Liriodendron tulipifera* (tulip tree), *Liquidambar styraciflua* (sweet gum) and *Gingko biloba* (maidenhair tree).

In the interim, turn left and follow a signed route to cross the road opposite the Mormon church. Follow the cycle track uphill for 300 metres before turning right into a depot. A fenced route leads to a new section of trail through Pontycafnau Iron Works and passes Pontycafnau bridge (turn right and cross the bridge for access to Cyfartha Castle). From here, the trail climbs to run parallel with the A470 before crossing the Cefn Coed viaduct. Continue past the Station Hotel and cross Cefn Coed High Street before turning left up to St John's Church where a narrow lane will be found to the left of the church wall. Follow this onto the bridge over the A465 where you will be standing on the trackbed of the former Brecon and Merthyr Railway. The old line provides a marvellously easy route of the next 3 miles.

A view at dusk from the eastern parapet of Cefn Coed viaduct (David James Photography (Sussex))

As you climb the gradient of Cefn Coed High Street, spare a thought for the electric trams which passed this way. The Merthyr Electric Traction and Lighting Company inaugurated tram services in April 1901 over a network linking Dowlais, Merthyr Tydfil and Cefn Coed. The services were initially very popular but, like the railways, lost passengers to rival buses between the wars. A particular problem was the need to renew the rails periodically, which involved digging up whole streets at a time. The track was last renewed in 1914, and the cost of repeating the exercise was a major reason for the closure of the system in August 1939. By this time the trams had become unpopular and were being subsidized by the company's profits on sales of electricity. Indeed, many locals wanted to see the roads made up to a proper standard, which could only be done if the tramlines were removed.

If you continue a few yards beyond the turning into Church Road, the Station Hotel is on the left at the end of a short cul-de-sac. Cefn Coed station once stood opposite, and a footpath now leads onto Cefn Coed viaduct (GR 031077). This is the larger of the two viaducts on the B&M's Merthyr branch, being 770 ft long and 115 ft high, with fifteen arches of 39 ft 6 in span; indeed, it is the third-largest viaduct in Wales. Looking east, one can clearly see Cyfarthfa Castle on the distant hillside; the Crawshays may have banished the railway to the far side of the Taf Fechan Valley, but they had a permanent view of Cefn Coed viaduct to remind them of its presence.

St John's Church was built between 1870 and 1874, just after the completion of Vaynor 'new' church (see below), with which it has much in common. Both buildings were designed by the Cardiff architect G.E. Robinson, built by David Jenkins of Merthyr, and supported financially by Robert Thompson Crawshay, last of the Cyfarthfa ironmasters. When Crawshay agreed to pay for the new church at Vaynor, the public had already subscribed some £700 for that purpose; Crawshay insisted that this money be transferred to the building of St John's, which was intended as a chapel of ease to the mother church he was financing. It served this role until 1925, when the new parish of Cefn Coed was formed. Unfortunately, the years have not been kind to St John's: it has undergone many alterations, the most severe of which was probably the installation of the Beatitudes Window in 1902. This necessitated the demolition of the original apse and three lancet windows, and some commentators have not been particularly kind about the result.

After crossing the Heads of the Valleys road, the Taff Trail begins the long climb to the old railway summit at Torpantau which, coincidentally, is also the summit of the modern cycle route. The line rises steadily on a gradient of 1 in 45–50, passing the backs of modern houses at Trefechan. The Taf Fechan Nature Reserve – an unspoilt habitat of woodland and limestone – lies on the opposite side of the valley, accompanied by the line of the old Gurnos Tramroad. This is another transport route associated with the Merthyr Tydfil iron industry, having been built in the 1800s to convey limestone to the Cyfarthfa ironworks. Vaynor Quarry lies

Pontsarn viaduct carried the Brecon and Merthyr Tydfil Joint Railway over the valley of the Taf Fechan. It is 455 ft long, 92 ft high and crosses the valley in seven spans of 40 ft 6 in. This section of the Taff Trail was opened by Prince Charles in July 1991 (author)

out of view to the left: despite the fact that rail traffic ceased in 1966, the quarry is still being worked and produces large quantities of roadstone.

The empty platform of Pontsarn station heralds the arrival of Pontsarn viaduct (GR 045099), which finally carries the line from the west to the east side of the valley. The line now curves around Morlais Hill, which is surmounted by the ruins of Morlais Castle (GR 049096). Given its commanding views, it is hardly surprising that Morlais Hill has been occupied since the Iron Age, when it was the site of a fort. The remains visible today date from a castle built in the 1280s by Gilbert de Clare, Earl of Gloucester. After a short but violent history, the castle was captured by the Welsh in 1314. It is last mentioned in the Civil War when it was seized by the Roundheads and burned. Nowadays, only ruins and earth banks remain, but in these can be traced the course of the outer wall and the sites of seven towers.

The tiny village of Vaynor lies to the north of the line. This was once the site of a medieval *meanor*, from which it takes its name, but it attracts most interest today for its churches (GR 048102). The original church was built in AD 874, destroyed in the Battle of Maes Y Faenor in 1286 (one of the many Anglo-Welsh conflicts at that time) and then rebuilt in its present form in 1291. The 'new' church next door has a less colourful history, having been built in 1870 by Robert Thompson Crawshay who lies buried in the grounds beneath a tablet of Radyr stone bearing the legend 'God Forgive Me'. He is reputed to have been a bully both to his workers and family, so this surprisingly humble inscription may be an attempt to make his peace with God.

The site of Morlais Junction lies at GR 057099, where LNWR trains left the Brecon and Merthyr Railway to pursue their own course over the Heads of the Valleys to Abergavenny. The site today is indicated by a widening of the formation accompanied by cliffs on the right and a solitary bench for weary walkers; it is easily missed. The line to Brecon then turns north and runs alongside the minor road from Pant to Pontsticill. The railway path finishes at GR 105061, where there is a small picnic area. The Taff Trail then takes to the lanes through Pontsticill.

> **On reaching the end of the railway path, turn left and proceed under a rail-over-road bridge at GR 060106. Continue straight ahead for half a mile to a Y-junction at GR 060113 and turn right. In just under half a mile, turn left and cross the dam of Pontsticill Reservoir, noting the lane to Pontsticill station straight ahead. The road then snakes uphill to join the minor lane from Pontsticill to Talybont at GR 057115. Turn right here and proceed north towards Talybont.**

Until the trail crosses Pontsticill Reservoir, the course of the B&M Merthyr branch can be seen to the right, with the former 'main' line to Dowlais running just beyond it higher up the hill. The Dowlais line now accommodates the 2 ft gauge Brecon Mountain Railway which operates between Pant and Pontsticill. This is one of the younger 'Great Little Trains of Wales', having opened on 8 June 1980. It has a collection of locomotives originating from East Germany and South Africa, and there are plans to extend northwards to Torpantau.

Pontsticill makes an attractive lakeside terminus for this little line and revives a connection between rail and water that flourished in the nineteenth century. Pentwyn Reservoir (a mile and a half to the north) was completed in 1862 to supply Merthyr and Dowlais with water, but its dam was built over a geological fault which leaked so much water that a new reservoir, Pontsticill, had to be built to the south. This was completed in 1927. The combined reservoirs now form an artificial lake 2$\frac{1}{2}$ miles long which holds up to 3,400 million gallons of water.

The popularity of Pentwyn Reservoir for recreation was established by the letting of boating and fishing licences, and the inauguration in 1863 of an annual Pentwyn Regatta. Most visitors to the regatta travelled by rail, using nearby

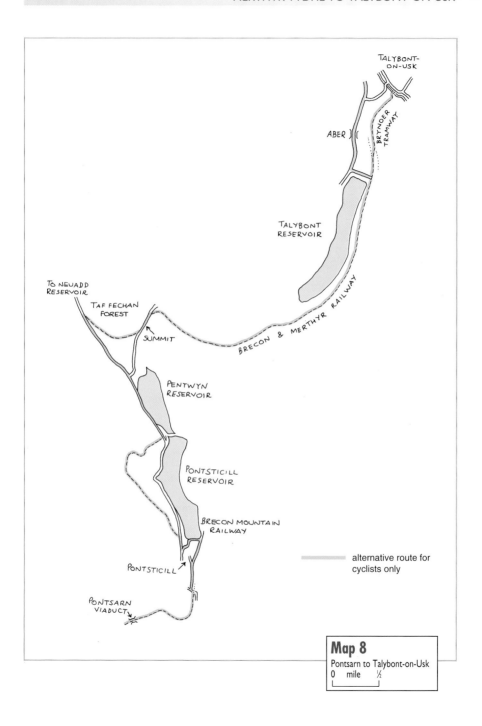

TALYBONT-
ON-USK

BRYNOER
TRAMWAY

ABER

TALYBONT
RESERVOIR

TO NEUADD
RESERVOIR

TAF FECHAN
FOREST

SUMMIT

BRECON & MERTHYR RAILWAY

PENTWYN
RESERVOIR

PONTSTICILL
RESERVOIR

BRECON MOUNTAIN
RAILWAY

alternative route for
cyclists only

PONTSTICILL

PONTSARN
VIADUCT

Map 8
Pontsarn to Talybont-on-Usk
0   mile   ½

In view of the fact that Prince Charles has been guest of honour at a Taff Trail function, it is appropriate that the locomotive hauling this 'Santa Special' on the nearby Brecon Mountain Railway should bear his name (David James Photography (Sussex))

Dolygaer station. Their numbers were so vast (6,000 in a single day in 1867) that the station had to be enlarged to cope. The reservoir even boasted a pleasure steamer, which suffered the ignominy of sinking during its first season. It was refloated and continued to work afterwards, the accident not affecting its popularity.

> The lane from Pontsticill to Talybont climbs gently uphill, with trees appearing first on the right and then on the left. About 30 yd after entering woodland completely, the trail forks left onto a wide forest track. This turning is at GR 057120 and is marked by a wooden finger board.
>
> Follow this path for a mile and a half to a waterfall on a stream (GR 045138), where the trail bears right and downhill through the forest. It rejoins the Pontsticill–Talybont lane at a point below Pentwyn dam (GR 054144). Turn left here and continue along the lane as far as a road junction at GR 054142, then proceed straight ahead, following the sign to Neuadd Reservoir.

This is the start of an uphill section of just under one and a half miles. A bridge over the Taf Fechan is crossed at GR 042163, followed by a picnic area with car park and toilets at GR 042163. About half a mile further on, turn sharp right onto a bridleway which runs gently downhill to a point above the southern portal of Torpantau tunnel (GR 049167). This is the third and final junction with the Pontsticill–Talybont lane.

Turn left here, then proceed uphill and over the summit of the trail at GR 052172. A quarter of a mile further on, turn right onto an unmetalled forestry road at GR 055174; this brings the trail back onto the course of the Brecon and Merthyr Railway, which it rejoins at the top of the famous Seven Mile bank. After the long slog from Merthyr, the next 7 miles will seem extremely easy!

Shortly after leaving Pontsticill, the trail enters a series of conifer plantations which end at Taf Fechan Forest, near the summit at Torpantau. The exposed summits in this area do not support a great variety of either plant life or agriculture, but the mountain sides have proved well suited to this particular form of arboriculture. The trees were originally planted by the water board, but the plantations have been managed for some years now by Forest Enterprise. Among the numerous spruce and fir it is still possible to find examples of the original oak, ash and alder.

Torpantau was one of the highest, coldest and loneliest places on a railway anywhere in the country. Given its location, a fairly substantial station was built with two platforms, a passing loop and a signal-box. The signal-box, opened in 1863 with the rest of the line, was not even provided with a fireplace until the staff petitioned the railway company to install one. This was done, grudgingly, in 1868. A similar request for sleeping accommodation was refused, even though snowdrifts often cut off the station from the outside world.

The most notable of these drifts occurred during the severe winter of 1947, when a passenger train from Brecon – with women and children on board – became stuck in Torpantau tunnel for several days. A rescue engine was sent to free it, but this was derailed by the sheer weight of snow packed onto the track. Jet engines

An unusual photograph of the overflow at Pontsticill Reservoir in full spate. The tower at the end of the footway sits atop a supply pipe leading to the industrial valley around Merthyr Tydfil (David James Photography (Sussex))

were then borrowed from the RAF, fixed onto a flat goods cart and started up in an attempt to blow away the snow, but this too failed. It was not until troops from Brecon were called in to dig the train out that it was finally freed.

Nowadays the station site is empty. The tunnel portal has been bricked up and only two grassy mounds remain to indicate where the platforms once stood. Local farmers use the space between them for sheep dipping.

> **The forest road curves round to the right and descends to join the former B&M trackbed at GR 056171 just beyond the northern portal of Torpantau tunnel. The old railway heads off on an east-south-easterly bearing but gradually curves round to the left until, near Talybont, it is heading due north. The dam at the north end of Talybont reservoir marks the point at which the route for cyclists and walkers diverges.**
>
> **Cyclists cross the dam, turning right onto the road to Talybont at the far end. Please take care as this road can be deceptively busy. After 1¼ miles, the trail forks left and then turns left onto the B4558, 1¾ miles further on.**
>
> **Walkers continue straight on after passing the dam. About half a mile further on look out for a clearing where a wide forest track forks away to the right (GR 108210). Follow this track uphill to a point where it crosses the course of the old Brynoer Tramway (GR 108213). Turn left at the tramway and follow it downhill, crossing the Brecon and Merthyr Railway for a final time via a bridge at GR 113224. Continue downhill until the Monmouthshire and Brecon Canal comes into view on the left. Cross the canal via White Hart bridge (GR 114225), then turn right for the village or left for the towpath to Brecon.**

The B&M's Seven Mile bank is constructed on a shelf cut into the hillside. In describing this section, the company's 1858 prospectus declared blithely that 'a good locomotive road can be obtained throughout' – a claim which you can put to the test by walking or cycling the other way! The first half-mile falls at 1 in 68, then the gradient steepens to 1 in 38 for the remaining 6½ miles. The total descent is 925 ft.

On a gradient of this unprecedented length, runaways were a major problem. Operating standards were gradually tightened to reduce the risks, but they did not prevent a spectacular crash on the night of 2 December 1878. Northbound trains were required to stop immediately north of Torpantau tunnel so that the guard could pin down the brakes on the wagons. On this ill-fated occasion he failed to do so. The crew's 37-wagon train was being hauled by no less than three locomotives, two at the front and one at the rear, so they must have assumed that the weight and power of the engines was sufficient to control the load. They were tragically wrong. The train soon began to accelerate out of control, so the drivers put their engines into reverse. Unfortunately, this had no effect but to shake them to pieces;

Just after passing the summit of the trail, the trackbed of the Brecon & Merthyr Railway is joined for a descent of the famous Seven Mile Bank. This is the view from near the top, overlooking Talybont Reservoir (author)

parts of their drive mechanisms were later found 2 miles from the foot of the bank, at a point now marked by the dam of Talybont Reservoir. By the time the train crossed the canal bridge near the White Hart, it was travelling at about 60 mph. Seconds later it ran onto a 16 ft embankment with a curve considered safe for 40 mph. It then left the rails and plunged to its destruction, with only two of the six enginemen surviving. At the inquest which followed, it transpired that the guard had worked over thirty-five hours in the two days previous – all for 22s (£1.10) a week.

In railway days, the views across the valley of the Afon Caerfanell were magnificent. They still are of course, but the increased height of the trees restricts what modern trail users can see. Fortunately, there are clearings near the top of the bank and at the north end of Talybont Reservoir which still allow these scenic splendours to be viewed.

Halfway down the bank stood the tiny halt of Pentir Rhiw, where the signalman also acted as ticket clerk. His passengers came from isolated farms in the valley which were submerged when the reservoir was formed in the 1930s. The station

A tranquil scene at Talybont on the Monmouthshire and Brecon Canal. The parapet on the right indicates the presence of an aqueduct over the fast-flowing Afon Caerfanell (author)

stood at GR 102184 just south of the modern adventure centre.

The 12 mile Brynoer Tramway was opened in May or June 1815, having been built by a small group of shareholders in the Brecknock and Abergavenny Canal, and Benjamin Hall, who owned a colliery at Brynoer, north of Rhymney. From Brynoer, the line climbed over the mountains to Trefil limestone quarries, then skirted around Cefn Crug before descending to Talybont on a shelf cut into the hillside. Traffic was mainly limestone from Trefil, plus pit props from Brecon and coal the other way. Much of the coal and limestone was transshipped to canal boats at Talybont, then conveyed by water to Newport. This was a very slow and circuitous route, so the tramway suffered from the opening of shorter and faster alternatives such as the Rumney Tramroad, which opened in 1836 and provided a direct route from Rhymney to Newport. The opening of the Brecon and Merthyr Railway dealt the *coup de grâce*, and by 1865 the tramway was moribund.

However, despite its early closure, the route of the tramway from Talybont to Trefil has been absorbed into the local bridleway network; it makes an interesting, if strenuous, walk. A notable feature is the survival of an impressive row of limekilns alongside the canal bank at Talybont wharf (GR 115224). Tramway wagons once ran along the top of these, discharging their loads into the burning-cones below. A recently restored wharf office, which once belonged to one of the tramway's bankers, stands nearby.

Talybont is a straggling village built alongside the B4558 and the lane to the former railway station (GR 117228). However, it boasts a good range of facilities, including public toilets (by the White Hart), a store and post office (complete with tearoom), bus services to Brecon and no fewer than three pubs. There is a busy livestock market on Thursdays, but the most dominant feature is the canal, the towpath of which provides the next section of the trail to Brecon.

5

TALYBONT-ON-USK TO BRECON

**7 MILES
EASY**
ORDNANCE
SURVEY MAPS
1:50,000 Landranger
Sheets 160 and 161
1:25,000 Outdoor Leisure
Map 11

THE MONMOUTHSHIRE & BRECON CANAL

Introduction

With the rigours of the mountain crossing now over, the Taff Trail finishes with a level section of 7 miles along the towpath of the Monmouthshire & Brecon Canal. Some writers regard this as the most beautiful canal in the country, which is hardly surprising when one considers that much of it follows the valley of the River Usk. However, the charm of the canal lies in more than reflected glory, especially east of Talybont where the river valley is narrow and the canal clings to a wooded ledge on its southern slope.

West of Talybont the river valley widens and this gives the canal a chance to meander along the contours, with rolling pastures to the north and impressive views of the Brecon Beacons to the south. The route naturally has much to offer in terms of aquatic wildlife, but there are also three aqueducts, four lift bridges and a lock to add interest – not to mention a number of weathered stone bridges which are so much a feature of waterways throughout the country. Between April and October many pleasure craft can be seen on the canal, some of them narrow boats brightly decorated with the traditional motifs of castles and roses.

The Taff Trail finishes at Brecon, which, strictly speaking, has been a city since its large priory church was granted cathedral status in 1923. More English than Welsh in appearance, Brecon is lucky in having escaped lightly at the hands of twentieth-century road builders and architects. Its streets are packed with history and it is easy to see why it is so popular with tourists.

Cyclists are no longer permitted to cycle on the canal towpath and have an alternative route to Brecon via Llanfrynach and Cantref, which follows minor roads and bridleways. This is steep in places and part of the bridleway section is rough (there is an alternative described on page 77), but the climb is rewarded with superb views, especially on the final descent to Brecon.

History

The present-day Monmouthshire and Brecon Canal actually began life as two separate canal companies: the Monmouthshire Canal, whose main line ran from Newport to Pontypool; and the Brecknock and Abergavenny Canal, which ran from Pontypool to Brecon. The two canals met at an end-on junction at Pontymoile basin in Pontypool. The Monmouthshire company was always the stronger concern, largely because it was well positioned to profit from the iron and coal industries which flourished in the South Wales valleys. However, by one of those ironies which so often appears in transport history, it is the Brecknock and Abergavenny Canal which remains in operation today. While much of the Monmouthshire remains intact (including its towpath), it survives purely as a water supply, and its many locks have been turned into weirs.

The Monmouthshire Canal appeared on the scene first, obtaining its Act in June 1792. Two months later, notices for the Brecknock and Abergavenny Canal were published, promoting a line from Newbridge, near Caerleon, to Gilwern; the decision to extend to Brecon was taken in December 1792. Had this scheme been adopted, the two canals would have ended up as rivals for the same trade south of Pontypool, but a compromise was reached whereby the Monmouthshire gave the B&A a £3,000 grant plus a supply of water in return for the latter constructing a line from Brecon to Pontymoile. It is believed that the Monmouthshire committee was responsible for this example of far-sighted co-operation.

Thomas Dadford Junior was appointed as engineer in October 1792 and instructed to make a 'Plan and Estimate' for the proposed canal, including three connecting tramways. His plans and estimates were accepted in November and an Act duly followed in March 1793. This gave the company powers to cut a 33 mile long canal, as well as connecting tramways up to 8 miles from the waterway. The combined use of rail and water was a feature of canals in south Wales generally: the promoters did not suspect that tramways would develop into railways and eventually steal their trade.

In the event, the Brecknock and Abergavenny Canal proved uncommonly keen on tramways and set about constructing an extensive network of these before beginning to cut the waterway that would join them all together. Even at the time, this must have been an unusual policy, for it certainly caused great irritation to the committee of the Monmouthshire Canal. On the plus side, the tramways gave the B&A an early source of income, but the Monmouthshire wanted its connection at Pontymoile, which the tramway policy clearly failed to provide. At one stage the Monmouthshire became so desperate to get things moving that it ordered its own engineer to stake out the B&A's line!

After several years of prevarication, the B&A finally began its cut at the beginning of 1797. The 8 mile section from Gilwern to Llangynidr is believed to have opened in November that year, followed by a further 3½ miles from Llangynidr to Talybont in February 1799. The canal finally reached Brecon on 24 December 1800, whereupon the price of coal fell by about 25–30 per cent, thus realizing one of the promoters' principal ambitions.

The main features on the Talybont to Brecon section were Ashford tunnel (just east of the Taff Trail) and the lock and four-arched aqueduct at Brynich. All were engineered by Thomas Dadford using local contractors.

On 14 January 1805 a further extension was opened from Gilwern to Govilon, but then the money ran out – 12 miles short of Pontymoile. Over the years that followed, the Monmouthshire protested with increasing vigour about the unfinished state of the B&A and even asked for the return of its £3,000 grant, which had been paid on condition that the two canals actually joined. The B&A gave a succession of evasive replies, finally prompting the Monmouthshire to take legal advice, which did the trick. In 1809 the B&A arranged a series of loans totalling £50,000, which enabled it to complete the link to Pontymoile. The principal lender was Richard Crawshay of Cyfarthfa who put up £30,000, apparently because a nephew needed the completed canal for transport to and from his works.

Under the circumstances, it is not surprising that the B&A constructed the final section of its waterway from Pontymoile northwards. The committee took an inaugural trip between the two canals on 7 February 1812, by which time the total cost of its combined canal and tramway system had reached something in excess of £200,000. This was £50,000 more than allowed for in the company's Act, but completion of the Pontymoile connection led to a rapid increase in revenue from tolls.

The company now began a period of relative prosperity, with dividends first being paid in 1807. Naturally there were peaks and troughs allied to the economic cycle, and there was also a period of damaging competition with the Monmouthshire. However, this was resolved and reasonable profits were sustained well into the 1840s.

By 1845 railway mania had arrived and the committee soon realized the way things were going. Between 1845 and 1860 several attempts were made to sell the canal while it was still worth something (there was even a scheme to lay a single-track railway along its bank) but none was followed by any successful action. By the early 1860s the impact of the railways was severe, with dividends falling from £6 per share in 1856 to 10s (50p) per share in 1862. By 1863 all of the local iron traffic and most of the coal had been lost to rail, and it became difficult to convene enough shareholders to elect a committee, let alone take responsible decisions. Finally, on 29 September 1865, the B&A sold out to the Monmouthshire Canal, which was still financially strong, having taken the decision to turn itself into a railway in 1845. The Monmouthshire wanted the B&A principally for the supply of water it drew from the Usk at Brecon, which it sold on to industrial customers south of Pontymoile. The Monmouthshire survived as a combined railway and canal company until 1875, when it was leased by the Great Western Railway. The GWR formally absorbed it on 1 August 1880, whereby the Brecknock and Abergavenny became yet another waterway owned – and largely unwanted – by a major railway company. It was the GWR, incidentally, which first applied the 'Monmouthshire and Brecon' title to the two canals.

By the turn of the century the only vessel travelling the whole length of the B&A was the weekly market boat from Newport, although two or three other boats worked on the upper part. The last toll was collected in February 1933 at Llangattock, near Crickhowell. The Monmouthshire Canal was abandoned by a series of Acts passed between 1930 and 1962, and it appears that the 1962 legislation abandoned the B&A as well. After this, the Brecon section was kept open as a water channel, but a number of 'awkward' structures were altered or

A level crossing on a canal? Improbable but true. Boaters are supplied with a key to the concrete hut behind the bridge, which houses an electric motor for lifting the span. Note the strange angle of the moored boats: after a period of prolonged heavy rain, the canal sluices had been opened to prevent the canal from flooding or bursting its banks (David James Photography (Sussex))

removed, such as the lift bridge at Talybont which was dismantled and replaced by a culvert.

Fortunately, two important new organizations were created at about this time: the Brecon Beacons National Park Authority and the British Waterways Board. Recognizing the recreational potential of the canal in the new national park, the BWB began restoration in 1964 with financial assistance from the then Brecon and Monmouth county councils. Work proceeded steadily until 1970, when a new lift bridge was installed at Talybont. This re-opened the whole length of the B&A for pleasure craft, but disaster struck five years later when a breach at Llanfoist led to closure of the central section pending a study into the canal's future. This found that a large injection of capital was necessary to remedy over fifty years' arrears of maintenance – far more than the impecunious BWB could afford to invest. The outlook appeared grim, but in 1977 sufficient funds were found to finance the rest of the restoration. The main contributors were the Welsh Development Agency and the Manpower Services Commission, which contributed £231,000 and £170,000 respectively. As a result, the entire line of the Brecknock and Abergavenny re-opened again in 1981, including a new aqueduct over the River Menascin east of Llanfrynach. The culmination of the campaign to restore the canal came in 1983, when the government finally removed the waterway's 'remainder' status and reclassified it as a cruising canal that should be retained in the inland waterway system.

Route Description

Note: Cycling is not permitted on the towpath of the Monmouthshire and Brecon Canal, except between Brynich Lock and Brecon, where a specially designed shared use path has been constructed. Cyclists must follow the route signed on country lanes between Talybont-on-Usk and Brynich Lock. (Described on p. 76).

(1) Walking route: Canal towpath via Pencelli and Brynich

> There are several places to join the canal towpath in Talybont, but the easiest are behind the White Hart Inn (GR 114225) or at Talybont lift bridge, which is an unmistakable landmark on the B4558 (GR 112227). The towpath follows the north side of the canal for the first 4 ½ miles, then changes banks at Twm bridge (No. 162), which is within sight of Brynich aqueduct.

The 'Mon and Brec' canal has been justly described as a 33 mile long nature trail. It is abundant in plant and animal life, although the latter has suffered in

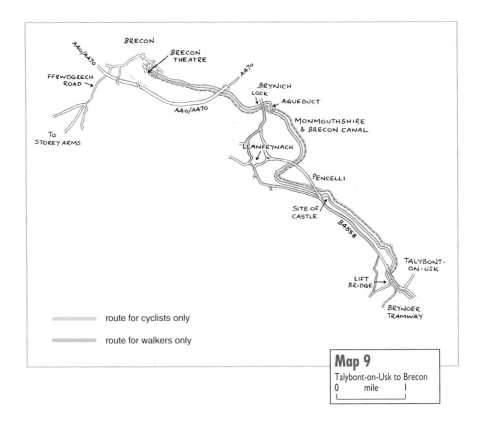

route for cyclists only

route for walkers only

Map 9
Talybont-on-Usk to Brecon
0   mile   I

recent years due to attacks by wild mink which were once farmed locally for their fur. Mallards and moorhens are common, but herons and kingfishers can also be seen; in fact, the canal is one of the few places where kingfishers breed. Good stocks of roach, perch and dace make the waterway an excellent coarse fishery, and east of Talybont, bream and mirror carp add to the variety; these last two species are a relatively recent introduction by British Waterways. At the Brecon end it is possible to see eels and even grass snakes swimming in the water.

Along the canal banks, a wide variety of trees and shrubs can be found. The alder is the most common species, but there are also plenty of oak, ash, hawthorn and sycamore. In autumn, wild raspberries, elderberries and blackberries provide an abundance of fruit, which is harvested both by humans and a variety of garden and woodland birds. These include tits, wrens, woodpeckers, nuthatches and treecreepers. In summer, swallows are a common sight, swooping low over the water to catch insects, as are bright blue damselflies, which use the canal for their aquatic nymph stage. Even the most casual observer can expect to spot the odd squirrel, frog or toad, and in autumn, squirrels frequently betray their presence with a scattering of empty hazelnut shells on the ground.

Picking up the towpath behind the White Hart, the trail begins with a cluster of engineering features, the first of which is an aqueduct over the Afon Caerfanell. Look out for the sluice at its south-west corner, which is used to control the water level during periods of heavy rain. Much of the canal in Talybont is built on an embankment and the sluice is an important means of preventing floods and breaches. (In the nineteenth century the Brecknock and Abergavenny company employed a molecatcher to keep the canal watertight!)

Before moving on, look back to the east and you will see two bridges: the first of these carried the Brynoer Tramway over the cut, while the second was built by the Brecon and Merthyr Railway. If you can spare the time, it is worth making a half-mile detour along this section to see the limekilns at Talybont wharf and the western portal of Ashford tunnel.

Continuing west, the next major feature is Talybont lift bridge, which was installed in 1970. This is electrically powered and operated by boat crews, who also have to close a set of level-crossing gates to road users. This is an unusual arrangement by any standards and particularly surprising for visitors to the area.

A row of cottages alongside the canal at Talybont. The two elderly gentlemen with the dog give the scene a timeless quality, which characterizes much of the canal as well (David James Photography (Sussex))

There are three more lift bridges on the canal between Talybont and Pencelli, but after the electrically powered bridge at Talybont, boaters will find these a little more demanding – they all have to be raised manually (author)

At GR 112230 the canal passes under the B4558 and reaches open country: it then begins a meandering curve along the contour lines before rejoining the road for a straight run to Pencelli. There are three more lift bridges along this section, again operated by boat crews, but this time they have to rely on muscle power.

At Pencelli the canal turns sharply to the left (GR 095250), before passing under the B4558 by a modern bridge. Watch out for this spot, for it marks the site of Pencelli Castle which once stood atop the mound on the south bank. Thomas Dadford ran the canal through two sides of the castle moat, probably saving half a day's labour by his army of navvies in the process. The castle was one of four local strongholds granted to Norman knights, but was abandoned in the Middle Ages due to its poor position and vulnerability to firearms. The site is now occupied by a farm, which includes several sections of original walling in its yard; it is not open to the public.

Beyond the roadbridge the canal turns to the right and passes the garden of the Royal Oak, bridge No. 154 and Pencelli wharf in quick succession. It then turns north-east, crossing the valley of the Nant Menascin on an embankment. The aqueduct at GR 083257 is a modern structure, having been rebuilt in the 1960s when the canal was closed. Nowadays it is the narrowest point on the cut but, despite the economy of reconstruction, boats with a beam of 8 ft can just squeeze through. Beyond the aqueduct on the north bank, the Storehouse is an eighteenth-century canalside warehouse: the owners run a tearoom, craft shop and horse-drawn trip boat. Having crossed the Nant Menascin, the canal again clings to the contours as it enters a narrow section of the Usk Valley where river and waterway are forced into close proximity.

Twm bridge is situated on a sharp right-hand bend in the canal at GR 079271. The towpath changes sides here, then crosses the River Usk via the four-arched Brynich aqueduct. In another 200 yd the canal passes under the B4558 by a bridge but the towpath crosses it on the level. Take care here, as this is a downhill stretch of road and cars may be travelling at speed. Beyond the road lies picturesque Brynich lock, complete with a small picnic area; the flower tubs around the lock chamber are a particular delight in summer.

The remaining 2 miles to Brecon are on an easy shared use path. The canal has recently been extended with the construction of a basin which provides a waterside frontage for the canal warehouse style Theatr Brycheiniog. The theatre marks the end of the Taff Trail in Brecon and is the perfect place to stop and contemplate your journey or reward your effort with refreshments.

To reach the centre of Brecon, follow the road round past the tall sculpture. Turn right at the mini roundabout into Rich Way. Continue staright on to a T-junction with The Watton and turn left. The route comes out in The Bulwark, just below St Mary's Church. Bus services depart from the nearby Wellington Hotel.

Brynich aqueduct is the third aqueduct on this section of the towpath and, while not the tallest on the canal, it is definitely the most impressive. It was engineered by Thomas Dadford and built between 1797 and 1800. An overflow weir at the south end controls the water level, while the aqueduct itself can be sealed off by the use of 'stop planks' and the water let out via a plug; the slots for the planks can be seen clearly at each end.

Brynich lock is the next major feature. It has a 10 ft drop and was restored to its present state in 1970. The chamber has a single gate at the top and double gates at

Brynich aqueduct is difficult to photograph, but offers an excellent view of the old packhorse bridge upstream on the River Usk (author)

Brynich lock, restored in 1970, is a memorable sight during the summer, with excellent displays of flowers. Here a party of schoolchildren waits to watch a boat pass through en route from Brecon to Talybont (Merthyr & Cynon Groundwork Trust)

the bottom, as is common, but is about 9 ft 6 in wide. This makes the B&A neither a conventional narrow (7 ft) nor a conventional broad canal (14 ft), but a 'narrow-ish' canal. This unusual gauge was standard on all the south Wales routes engineered by Dadford and his relatives (his brother John, and father Thomas senior, were other notable canal engineers of the period). To complete the scene, Brynich lock has a stone bridge at the east end. This is another example of normal practice, for a bridge built below the drop was easier to design and required fewer building materials.

West of Brynich the canal occupies a ledge above the fast-flowing River Usk, which lies at the foot of a steep bank covered in bracken – a colourful sight in autumn. By the time it passes under the busy A40 (GR 066277), the canal has curved away from the river to join the B4601, which it then accompanies all the way to Brecon. The waterway enters the town by the back door, passing a succession of pretty canalside gardens with overhanging trees. Unfortunately, the infilling of Brecon basin and the short section leading to it has created a rather drab terminus. Gas Works bridge and the nearby cottage are attractive, but the area beyond is an example of how not to reclaim a former industrial site: the backs of nearby industrial and commercial properties overlook what is little more than a dusty, unmade car park. The local authorities are actively considering major improvements to this area which, if implemented, would present a more inviting image to canal-borne visitors.

That aside, the rest of Brecon is a delight, with many fine buildings and places of interest. The town has been the administrative centre of the Brecon uplands since Roman times, and although little of Roman origin remains, the narrow streets and passageways give parts of the place a distinctly medieval flavour. A town trail guide can be purchased from the Tourist Information Centre in the car park north of the Bulwark and this is a wise investment for anyone who wants to explore the town more thoroughly. The TIC also acts as a National Park Information Centre, which is handy if you intend to explore the Brecon Beacons while staying in the area.

The cathedral, situated on the bank of the Afon Honddu, used to be the priory church of St John the Evangelist. It was built in the thirteenth and fourteenth

The Castle Hotel in Brecon occupies an imposing position overlooking the confluence of the rivers Usk and Honddu. The castle, seen on the right, was ruined during the Civil War by townspeople who wanted neither side to gain control. It has been recognized in recent years that there were three sides in the Civil War: the Roundheads, the Royalists and the Neutrals, as is made evident here (David James Photography (Sussex))

centuries on the site of an earlier Norman church, but gradually fell into disrepair. It was restored in the 1870s and granted cathedral status in 1923. One unusual feature is that the bells in its tower cannot be rung: the tower is the oldest part of the building and is considered too weak to withstand regular bell-ringing. The interior has a Norman font, a fine Early English chancel arch and impressive vaulting. The Cordwainers' Chapel contains a stained-glass window depicting members of the families who held the Lordship of Brecknock, while the Havard Chapel is dedicated to the South Wales Borderers Regiment, which still figures prominently in the town.

Brecon Castle has fared less well in the twentieth century, for it is now bisected by a modern road. Part of the frontage remains attached to the Castle Hotel, which occupies an imposing site overlooking the confluence of the Usk and Honddu rivers, while the ruined Ely Tower is stranded in private grounds on the other side of Castle Square. The fortification was originally built by the Norman lord, Bernard Newmarch. It was reduced to its present state during the Civil War, when the townspeople – who wanted neither side to control it – helped to destroy it. An impressive view can be obtained from Llanfaes Bridge with the river and Promenade in the foreground. The Promenade is an attractive riverside walk which leads past the town weir to a boathouse and recreation ground. If you have time, you can continue along the bank for another mile to Fennifach.

Christ College is Brecon's public school. The original institution was founded by Henry VIII in 1541 and built on the site of the thirteenth-century priory of St Nicholas. The school survived until the early nineteenth century, when it declined and fell into disrepair. For a time its buildings were used as stables by farmers attending Brecon market, but a charter for a new school was granted in 1853 and it is this which stands on the south bank of the Usk today. Most of the present buildings are Victorian 'mock Gothic', but a few of the originals survive, including the chapel and refectory. These are not open to the public but viewings can be arranged by application to the headmaster.

Brecon also supports two museums. The Brecknock Museum is the more central of these, being housed in the former Shire Hall in Captain's Walk, a short distance from the canal terminus. The building was constructed in 1842 and includes a Victorian Assize Court, where Breconshire Quarter Sessions were held until 1971; the courtroom has been preserved much as it would have appeared at the end of the last session. The museum also contains exhibits and displays on local wildlife, arts and crafts, archaeology and social history. One of the domestic exhibits is a re-creation of a traditional Welsh kitchen, including a large collection of love spoons, once used as a symbol of betrothal. The museum is open throughout the year and admission is free.

The South Wales Borderers' Museum, situated next to the Barracks off The Watton, is something of a contrast. This is a military museum which chronicles the

A frosty morning at Christ's College, Brecon. Despite its apparent antiquity, most of the buildings are Victorian, the originals having fallen into disuse and disrepair in the early years of the nineteenth century (David James Photography (Sussex))

history of the regiments based in Brecon: the South Wales Borderers, the Monmouthshire and, in recent years, the Royal Regiment of Wales. They have won more Victoria Crosses than any other line infantry regiment in the British Army. The South Wales Borderers are probably best known for their heroic defence of the mission station at Rorke's Drift, when 141 Welsh soldiers held off 4,000 Zulu warriors, a feat commemorated in the film *Zulu*. The museum is packed with military memorabilia, including medals, uniforms, armaments and paintings. It is open from April to October.

Apart from these historical features, Brecon has a variety of other attractions. There is a bustling livestock market every Tuesday and Friday, and even if onlookers cannot understand the rapid patter of the auctioneers, it is still an event full of atmosphere. However, the most notable occasion in the town's calendar has to be the Brecon Jazz Festival, held annually in August. Apart from the obvious music-making, the festival provides an opportunity to consume a fair amount of ale and Welsh whisky, which is produced in the town. Unfortunately, there are no tours or free samples at the distillery, so those who seek the local *chwisgi* must buy it in pubs or hotel bars.

(2) Cycling route: Lanes and bridleways via Llanfrynach

This alternative route is intended for cyclists. Leave Talybont on the B4558 heading west (follow the signs to Brecon). The road follows the canal for 2 miles and you can often catch glimpses of it through the hedges, especially around Cross Oak where the three lift bridges are prominent. Shortly after entering Pencelli, turn left into a narrow lane (GR 094248) signposted to Llanfrynach before crossing the canal (if you pass the pub you've gone to far). This climbs uphill for just over a mile, then curves to the right and drops down to the village, which nestles in the valley of the Nant Menascin. In winter, farm vehicles can make this lane very muddy and slippery, so care may be needed.

Llanfrynach is an attractive village which has developed around a central square by the church. Its name may give some insight into its origin, for 'Llan' usually denotes a religious site, while 'Frynach' may be a corruption of Brynach, who was a local missionary in the fifth century. The site certainly has a very long history, including a period of Roman occupation which was made evident by the discovery of mosaics and a villa bathhouse in 1775. Unfortunately, none of these discoveries can be viewed here, but one of the mosaics is on display at the National Museum of Wales in Cardiff. Of more immediate interest to modern visitors is the White Swan, a public house dating from the thirteenth century which offers real ale and food. The pub has featured for many years in guides by Egon Ronay and the Consumers' Association, and its garden is reputed to be the best for miles.

Much of Llanfrynach church dates from the nineteenth century, although the fourteenth-century western tower has been retained. The memorials and graves commemorate several members of the Games family of Penkelly (sic) Castle, as well as many de Wintons. The de Wintons appeared in 1839, when a branch of the Wilkins family of Brecon changed its name. The Wilkinses were famous as Brecon bankers. Their business was founded in 1778 by Walter and Jeffreys (sic) Wilkins, who had returned from India with a fortune. They invested in every important canal scheme in South Wales except the Monmouthshire and, as a result, numbered many canal companies among their clients. The de Wintons appear to have favoured the railways, and John Parry de Winton was influential in the early history of the Brecon and Merthyr Railway as a director and early chairman of the company.

On entering the village, aim for the church, which is surrounded by a stone wall and turn left (GR 075257). Continue straight on for about ¾ of a mile, and turn left at a T-junction to rejoin the B4558 (GR 075267). A short downhill section brings you to Brynich bridge, which like the aqueduct to the right, spans the River Usk. Take care here as there is a directional priority system for vehicles on this bridge. Immediately after the bridge, turn left to leave the road and join the canal towpath at Brynich Lock.

The next two miles are on a traffic free path with views of the Brecon Beacons and surrounding countryside. This section of trail was opened in 1998 and has been designed for wheelchair users, walkers and cyclists. A friendly warning of your approach to other users will do much to ensure positive responses to the development of shared use routes in the future. The route is straightforward, passing under the A470 via a tunnel with a narrow walkway (cyclists must dismount here).

As you approach Brecon, the trail forks left to leave the towpath and join an access road. The reward is a magnificent set of limekilns to your right. Continue straight on, passing Brecon Hunt Kennels to your left. Shortly after passing Ty Camlas Bunkhouse the trail rejoins the towpath for a short distance. After passing a row of canal side cottages, bear left to leave the towpath and join a minor road which leads to the theatre. The road swings round to the left and then right to bring you to the Taff Trail relief map sculpture which, with the canal side sculpture by Michael Fairfax mark the end of the Taff Trail in Brecon.

6

BRECON TO CEFN COED VIA STOREY ARMS

THE BRECON BEACONS

16 MILES
MODERATI
ORDNANCE
SURVEY MAPS
1:50,000 Landranger
Sheet 160
1:25,000 Outdoor Leisu
Map II and Pathfinder
Sheet 1109

Introduction

Between Brecon and Cefn-Coed-y-Cymmer the Taff Trail offers two alternatives: the main cycling route via Talybont and Torpantau; or the mountain route via Storey Arms and Garwnant Forest Centre. This chapter describes the latter. It is extra to the main trail and was developed initially so that walkers could complete circular walks beginning and ending at Merthyr Tydfil, which is better served by public transport than Brecon. On the assumption that readers will follow the main trail northwards (see Chapters 4 and 5), this chapter is written in a southerly direction.

Whereas the main route is full of transport history, this alternative route is primarily a mountain trail which offers more to the natural historian. The scenery is especially fine, with much of the surrounding countryside owned by the National Trust. The route begins with a steady climb up the valley of the Afon Tarell, dominated by sheep farming, then picks up the old coach road to Storey Arms. South of Storey Arms it crosses the busy A470 then runs along the west side of a chain of reservoirs before reaching the ancient woodlands of Penmoelallt Nature Reserve. Beyond Penmoelallt it descends into the valley of the Afon Taf Fawr, which it follows as far as Cefn Coed where it joins the main Taff Trail to Merthyr Tydfil.

Originally, this route was developed solely for walkers, but the establishment of a cycle-hire facility at Garwnant has led to improvements and changes. Currently, cyclists can use the trail – or something close to it – from Brecon to Storey Arms, and again from Garwnant to Cefn Coed. However, there is currently no off-road cycling route between Storey Arms and Garwnant. This may change in the future but, at present, the only link is the A470 – if you decide to cycle along this busy road, please take care. Directions for both the walking and cycling routes are provided, but the cycling route was a very late addition. As a result, the general narrative describes the walking route only.

Route Description

The mountain route to Cefn Coed starts at Llanfaes Bridge in the centre of Brecon at GR 043286. Proceed west into Bridge Street, which becomes successively Orchard Street, Church Street and Newgate Street. At GR 035282 turn left into Ffrwdgrech Road, which passes under the A470 at GR 035281.

Follow Ffrwdgrech Road as far as GR 028273, where it fans out in three separate directions: follow the middle route as far as Waterfall Cottage at GR 021264. At Waterfall Cottage, there is a choice of route:

(1) If you are walking, turn right, proceed along the south side of the cottage, cross the small stream (Nant Cwm Llwch), then proceed north-west for a short distance before climbing the hillside on your left. The trail now runs south-west for about a mile over a series of stiles rejoining the lane at GR 007251.

(2) If you are cycling, carry on past Waterfall Cottage, bearing left as the road climbs a steep hill. Stay on the lane as far as a turning at GR 014256 and there turn right. Proceed straight ahead at the crossroads at GR 011253 and rejoin the walking route a quarter of a mile further on at GR 008251.

Waterfall Cottage is aptly named, with waterfalls on the Nant Cwm Llwch to both front and rear. The owner is evidently a carpenter, for apart from making house signs (a selection of which are displayed at the front of the property), he has also built a water wheel to harness the stream's power.

Having joined the footpath beyond the cottage, walkers can view the surrounding countryside, which is often obscured by the high-sided local lanes. The views are extensive, although the gently sloping sides of the valley disguise the fact that this is mountain terrain. Sheep farming is the mainstay of agriculture in this area, the main breed being the hardy Welsh Mountain Cross Cheviot. The only

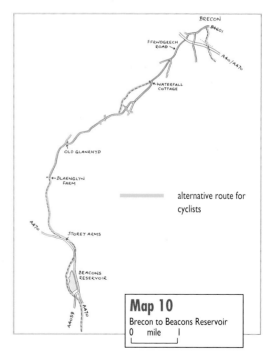

alternative route for cyclists

Map 10
Brecon to Beacons Reservoir
0   mile   I

Waterfall Cottage at Pont-rhyd-goch is aptly named, with waterfalls to both front and rear. This is a fall on the Nant Cwm Llwch which flows into the Afon Tarell (David James Photography (Sussex))

other animal strong enough to withstand the harsh winters here is the Welsh mountain pony.

Sheep have long been important in upland Wales, not only for their wool but also as a source of skins, meat, milk and manure. Mutton or lamb was frequently used in *cawl*, a meat and vegetable broth which provided the mainstay of the diet in rural Wales, while sheep milk was often made into cheese. This rich-flavoured delicacy remained available in Brecon market until the late 1940s. In the Middle Ages sheep were grazed on common land during the day but penned into arable fields at night, so that they fertilized the soil by treading their droppings into it.

The walking route passes a number of remote hillside farms on this section, whose rugged stone architecture suggests that they have to withstand some severe winter weather. The last of these farms, Gron-felen at GR 008252, has a stone-built privy in the yard, which recalls the basic standards that existed on these farms within living memory.

At GR 008251 walkers should turn right and cyclists proceed straight ahead, following the lane for just under a mile and a half to a T-junction at Old Glanrhyd (GR 984240). Turn left

With so much water power in the vicinity, the obvious course of action is to harness it. The mountain section of the Taff Trail fords the stream behind Waterfall Cottage and offers walkers a chance to view the owner's water wheel (David James Photography (Sussex))

The course of the trail looking north from Storey Arms towards Brecon. The A470 occupies the ledge on the far side of the valley, while the mountain pastures in the foreground are used by local sheep farmers (author)

here on to the old coach road to Storey Arms. This is a metalled road as far as Blaenglyn Farm (GR 977227), continuing thence as a rough track to Storey Arms (GR 982203).

There are more fine views along this section of the trail, with Afon Tarell to the right and the peak of Craig Cerrig-gleisiad (a national nature reserve) dominating the western skyline. After a period of heavy rain the Afon Tarell can be heard for some distance, sounding more like a waterfall than a stream. Blaenglyn Farm is another sheep farm, where the shepherd and his collie have mechanized their occupation and travel about the farm on a motorized buggy; they may bump past you on the track, to be seen later bringing in the sheep on the far side of the valley.

The paucity of human habitation in this area – all of it National Trust land – is very noticeable, so it is perhaps surprising to see an attractive white building nestling among the trees in the far distance on your right. This is Llwyn-y-celyn Youth Hostel (GR 973225), which can be reached via a connecting footpath which joins the trail just south of Blaenglyn Farm. The hostel is a former farmhouse which offers class 1, i.e. basic, accommodation.

At present, the next five miles of the trail are suitable for walkers only. On reaching Storey Arms, continue along the left-hand side of the A470 for just under half a mile passing the toilet block on your right-hand side, where you cross two stiles. At GR 987195 cross the road to the west side, proceed down the bank, over a stile and footbridge, then cross a stream at GR 987195. Walk around the edge of the plantation on the west side of Beacons Reservoir until you reach a stile, climb over and join the Forest Enterprise track, where you turn right. At the end of the track cross the A4059 Neath road at GR 988180.

Despite its name, Storey Arms is not a public house, nor is it open to the public. It is, in fact, an outdoor education centre which takes its name from a former inn which stood on the layby to the south. The only public provisions nowadays are a small car park, a bus stop and a telephone box, but half a mile to the south the trail passes a second car park which includes a picnic area and public toilets.

The section of trail from the A470 around the west side of Beacons Reservoir is a new addition to the local footpath network, having been completed in mid-1993. Beacons Reservoir is the first of three reservoirs in the Taf Fawr Valley, and was opened in 1897. Like Cantref and Llwyn-On reservoirs to the south, it was constructed to supply Cardiff with clean water. Earlier supplies in the city were unsanitary, giving rise to serious cholera epidemics in the 1840s and '50s. No less than thirty farms lie buried beneath these massive artificial lakes, and restrictions on the use of fertilizers, drainage and livestock farming – all to keep the water pure – dealt a blow to local farming from which it never fully recovered.

Another view in the vicinity of Storey Arms, again looking north towards Brecon, but note the change in the weather! Much of the land in the Brecon Beacons National Park is over 2,000 ft above sea level, so winter snows are quite common (Merthyr & Cynon Groundwork Trust)

South of the A4059 the trail continues via a track on the west bank of the Taf Fawr. At GR 989174 it passes into open country, re-entering woodland at GR 990166. It then continues south along a wide forest track for just under a mile to GR 992153, where it turns sharp left and descends to the dam at the south end of Cantref Reservoir

(GR 996153). If you wish to visit Nant Ddu Lodge you will have to leave the trail here: proceed across the dam to the main road, turn right and the lodge will be found in half a mile on your right at GR 002150.

For a mile south of Cantref dam the trail continues on the west side of the Taf Fawr, hugging the edge of the forest. On reaching a stile and gate turn right. At GR 003139 the trail meets a bridleway at a T-junction, where it turns right, climbing uphill for100 yd to GR 002139, where it turns left. It then passes the derelict buildings of Wern Farm at GR 001137, continuing to Garwnant Forest Centre at GR 003131.

By this point on the trail, conifer plantations have become commonplace. Most of these were planted in the 1950s and early '60s and are now managed by Forest Enterprise. Some of the older plantations have been felled on reaching maturity and are being restocked. Spruce, larch and pine account for most of the production, with only 7 per cent of the land being given over to minor species, including broad-leaved varieties. Timber harvested from these plantations is sent to mills throughout the country, which in turn manufacture a wide range of wood-based products: boards for the construction industry, garden furniture, sheds, fencing, chipboard and pulp for paper.

Nant Ddu Lodge (GR 002150) was originally a shooting lodge for the Morgan family of Tredegar, later providing accommodation for officials of the water board when the local reservoirs were being constructed. It is now a comfortable hotel set in attractive grounds, offering bar meals and drinks (including tea and coffee) to non-residents. Unfortunately, the Taff Trail and lodge are on opposite sides of the Taf Fawr, but it is hoped that an old bridge connecting the two will soon be restored. Until then, follow the directions given above.

South of Nant Ddu Lodge you may be surprised to find yourself walking on what looks like part of an old railway trackbed, visible as a slight mound in the grass. This is part of the old navvies' line, which ran from Penmoelallt quarry to Cantref dam. It was used intermittently between about 1890 and 1926, but has now mostly been absorbed into forest tracks.

Garwnant Forest Centre is a popular facility run by Forest Enterprise which attracts about 60,000 visitors each year. It has been carefully designed to maintain the character of the old farm buildings from which it was constructed. Its main feature is an exhibition and audio-visual programme which explains how forestry, farming and water supply have shaped the local landscape, but there is also a popular children's playground. There are many well-signposted walks in the vicinity and, in spring 1993, a cycle-hire facility was launched.

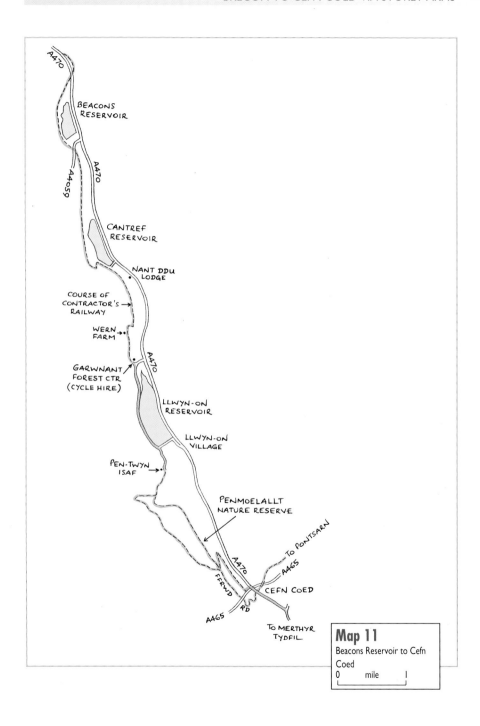

Map 11
Beacons Reservoir to Cefn Coed
0   mile   1

South of Garwnant Forest Centre the main access road swings sharp left but the trail bears right, dropping steeply downhill to join the lane on the west side of Llwyn-on Reservoir at GR 003129. It then follows this lane for a mile to the west end of Llwyn-on dam at GR 009112.

From Llwyn-on dam the trail continues south via the lane to Pen-twyn-isaf (GR 010108). At Pen-twyn-isaf the lane becomes a rough track which you should follow as far as GR 010106. Turn right here, following the wide forest track as it climbs uphill on to the wooded slopes of Penmoelallt. At GR 008102, there is a choice of route:

(1) If you are walking, turn left on to the narrow woodland path leading uphill; the junction is easily missed, so take care. You need to be an experienced walker to manage the next section as it twists and turns up the hillside. Fortunately the waymarking is fairly good, much of it in the form of large yellow dots painted on to tree turnks. If you take care to follow these, you will not get lost. The trail eventually joins a track along Craig Penmaillard, which runs gently downhill as far as the entrance to Penmoelallt Nature Reserve at GR 020088. South of the nature reserve, the trail follows a track to a point near Ffrwd Uchaf at GR 023085.

(2) If you are cycling, proceed straight ahead and follow the main forest track uphill as far as GR 003101. Turn sharp left here on to another track – still uphill – and follow this as far as a T-junction with a bridleway at GR 008099. Turn right at the T-junction and, 200 yards later, you will have passed the summit. Follow the bridleway downhill, passing Penmoelallt Farm en route at GR 021085. The cycling route rejoins the walking route just south of Penmoelallt Nature Reserve at GR 023085.

Llwyn-on is the most recent of the reservoirs in the Taf Fawr Valley, having been completed in 1926. It was originally scheduled for completion in 1915, but the outbreak of the First World War forced a long postponement. It is an attractive reservoir, flanked by a mature conifer plantation and well stocked with high-quality brown and rainbow trout.

It is a long, hard climb to Pen-twyn-isaf, but the reward is a fine view of the distant Taff Valley. A visit here just after sunrise on a crisp winter's morning is an experience not to be forgotten. When I visited, a forest plantation had just been cleared and even the sawdust had frozen hard as iron. The low sun was just dissolving the mist over the valley. There was not a soul about – not even the farm dog had stirred – and the only sound was the muted crunch of my boots against the frozen earth.

The walking route through Penmoelallt Nature Reserve may be uneven in places, but the variety of its trees offers a welcome contrast to the uniformity of what has gone before. The reserve is a natural limestone woodland of great importance, due to the presence of Ley's whitebeam (*Sorbus leyanus*). This tree grows on both sides of Cwm Taff – the name of the valley here – but nowhere else in the world. Another whitebeam, *Sorbus rupicola*, is unusual in that some specimens in the reserve have reached a height of over 30 ft, three times their normal height on other sites. Both species can be found on the ledges and cliff areas of the reserve.

Elsewhere, the tree cover is less exceptional but attractively varied, with ash, hazel, lime, rowan, silver birch and wych elm providing the main species. This diversity has produced a good range of woodland birds and spring flowers, the latter flourishing before the summer canopy of leaves has formed. The reserve is managed jointly by Merthyr Naturalists Society and Forest Enterprise.

South of Penmoellalt Nature Reserve the walking and cycling routes separate again. These directions begin at GR 022085 near Ffrwd Uchaf.

(1) If you are walking, turn sharp left (north) and follow the trail downhill as far as GR 021088. Turn sharp right here and follow the west bank of the Afon Taf Fawr (passing under the A470) as far as GR 027080, where the path crosses to the east bank via a footbridge. The trail then runs south as far as the A465 Heads of the Valleys road (GR 028079), turning left then right through the subway (GR 290079). Follow the road until it takes a sharp left turn, then right 100 yards further on and continue until you reach the Millennium milepost sculpture, marking the junction with the alternative route north and route south. Turn left passing in front of the Station Hotel to complete the circuit north and back to Brecon or right to cross the viaduct for the route into Merthyr Tydfil and to continue the trail south to Cardiff.

(2) If you are cycling, turn left and downhill to pass under the A470 and immediately right to follow the bridleway which joins Ffrwd Road. Follow this to pass under Cefn Coed viaduct with a steep pull uphill before turning sharp left to join the walking route into Cefn Coed. At the Millennium milepost sculpture turn left to complete the circuit north to Brecon via Talybont-on-Usk or right to cross the viaduct for the route south to Cardiff.

The trail is now fast approaching the start of the South Wales coal measures, where agriculture gave way to industry. A modern office block visible in the distance declares that civilization is not far away, but the view to the north is still impressive, with the rugged edge of Darren Fawr overhanging the A470 below.

The last part of the walking route along the river is an attractive stretch, with Cefn Coed cemetery situated on the hillside above to the right. This is a tidy and well-kept site providing the last resting place of what Kevin Littlewood calls the 'shopocracy' of nineteenth-century Merthyr: butter merchants, publicans, brewers, solicitors, and so on. The largest memorial is to Sir William Thomas Lewis, Baron Merthyr of Senghenydd, whom we last met in Chapter 3. A Jewish cemetery lies on the opposite bank of the river, purchased from a neighbouring farm by subscription in the 1860s.

A view from Storey Arms towards Brecon (Merthyr & Cynon Groundwork Trust)

On reaching Cefn Coed High Street, look out for the Station Hotel which is situated at the end of a short cul-de-sac on the south side (GR 031079). Cefn Coed viaduct, illustrated on the cover, lies just beyond and is worth close inspection. It is hoped that, eventually, the main trail will follow this part of the old Brecon and Merthyr Railway to Rhydycar (see Chapter 3), but a new road has been proposed south of here and the course of the cycle trail cannot easily be changed until this is complete.

If you have completed the entire trail, you have now covered 71 miles since leaving Cardiff – no mean achievement. En route you will have seen some of the extraordinary history of this part of South Wales and, hopefully, enjoyed some outstanding scenery. We hope that you have enjoyed the Taff Trail, will visit it again and recommend it to your friends. Furthermore, if you value this type of amenity, why not write to your local council and enquire what plans they have to create similar trails in your own locality?

APPENDICES

A. Transport Information

British Rail Telephone Enquiry Bureau
National Rail Enquiries   0345 484950
Valley lines   Cardiff (01222) 231978

Cardiff is well served by trains on the InterCity network. The Cardiff–Merthyr Tydfil line has an hourly service Monday–Saturday and a two-hourly service on Sunday. Bicycles are carried free of charge at off-peak times on this service, subject to the availability of space.

Brecon Mountain Railway
Enquiries to Brecon Mountain Railway, Pant Station, Dowlais, Merthyr Tydfil, CF48 2UP. Telephone Merthyr Tydfil (01685) 384854. The railway operates from Easter to the end of October, with a service of 'Santa Specials' over the Christmas period.

AA Services
Travel Information   0345 500600 (charged at local rate)
Emergency Service   0800 887766 (free)

RAC Services
Travel Information   0345 333222 (charged at local rate)
Emergency Service   0800 828282 (free)

Environmental Transport Association
Britain's only road rescue/breakdown organisation which campaigns for greener transport. The ETA also offers a cycle rescue service.
For further information quote ref. S110, ETA, Weybridge, Kent, KT13 8BR. Telephone Weybridge (01932) 828882.

Cycle Hire
Cyfartha Bike Hire, Cyfartha Castle, Merthyr Tydfil. Telephone Merthyr Tydfil (01685) 371555. Open daily 10 a.m. to 6 p.m. and most bank holidays Easter to October.

Garwnant Visitor Centre Cycle Hire, Cwm Taf, Merthyr Tydfil. Telephone Merthyr Tydfil (01685) 723060. Open all year 9 a.m. to 6 p.m. and later by arrangement.

Taff Trail Cycle Hire, Pontcanna Caravan Park, Pontcanna Fields, Cardiff CF1 9JJ. Telephone Cardiff (01222) 398362. Open 10 a.m. to 6 p.m. April to October.

Bus Operators

A complete list of buses and operators serving the Taff Trail is given below, but this is liable to change at short notice. Readers are therefore advised to check current arrangements with bus operators listed below.

Summary of Buses Serving the Taff Trail

Note: Sunday services are printed in italics

Cardiff Bus, Leckwith Depot, Sloper Road, Cardiff, CF1 8AF. Telephone Cardiff (01222) 396521.

26   Cardiff (Bus Stn) – Whitchurch – Tongwynlais – Taff's Well – Nantgarw – Caerphilly – Tredegar. Joint service with Islwyn Borough Transport. Hourly Monday–Saturday; *two-hourly Sunday.*

126   Cardiff (Central Railway Stn) – North Road – Gabalfa Interchange – Tongwynlais – Castell Coch (Gates). Five journeys daily Monday–Friday.

33A   Cardiff (Bus Stn) – Radyr – Morganstown – Tongwynlais – Castell Coch (Gates). Generally two hourly Monday–Saturday.

Many Cardiff Bus services operate locally within the city. Timetables are available for a small charge from the above address.

Islwyn Borough Transport, Penmaen Road Depot, Pontllanfraith, Blackwood, Gwent, NP2 2DL. Telephone Blackwood (01495) 226622.

16   Pontypridd (Bus Stn) – Cilfynydd – Quaker's Yard – Treharris – Nelson – Blackwood. Hourly Monday–Saturday.

26   Cardiff (Bus Stn) – Whitchurch – Tongwynlais – Taff's Well – Nantgarw – Caerphilly – Tredegar. Joint with Cardiff Bus. Hourly Monday–Saturday; *two-hourly Sunday (Sunday services operated by Glyn Williams).*

Johns Travel, 19 Six Bells Estate, Heolgerrig, Merthyr Tydfil, CF48 1TU. Telephone Merthyr Tydfil (01685) 373765.

Abercanaid – Merthyr Tydfil (Bus Stn). Generally half-hourly Monday–Saturday.

Stagecoach Rhondda, Aberhondda Road, Porth, CF39 0LN. Telephone Porth (01443) 682671.

X8   Cardiff (Bus Stn) – A470 – Pontypridd – Porth – Maerdy. Hourly Monday–Saturday.

C18/C19 Caerphilly (Bus Stn) – Nantgarw – Upper Boat – Rhydfelin – Pontypridd (Precinct). Every fifteen minutes Monday–Saturday, operated jointly with Shamrock.

132   Cardiff (Bus Stn) – Whitchurch – Tongwylais – Taff's Well – Nantgarw – Upper Boat – Rhydfelin – Pontypridd (Bus Stn) – Porth – Maerdy. Half-hourly Monday–Saturday; *generally two-hourly Sunday.*

Shamrock (Jones Motors), 34 Taff Street, Pontypridd, CF37 4TR. Telephone Pontypridd (01443) 409966/407000.

Cardiff (Bus Stn) – Tongwynlais –Taff's Well – Nantgarw – Upper Boat – Rhydfelin – Pontypridd (Bus Stn) – Abercynon – Aberdare. Half hourly Monday–Saturday.

Cardiff (Bus Stn) – A470 – Pontypridd (Bus Stn) – A470 – Abercynon – Mountain Ash – Aberdare. Hourly Monday–Saturday; *generally two-hourly Sunday after 2 p.m.*

Caerphilly (Bus Stn) – Nantgarw – Upper Boat – Rhydfelin – Pontypridd (Precinct). Hourly Monday–Saturday.

Pontypridd (Bus Stn) – A470 – Nelson – Treharris – Bedlinog. Half-hourly Monday–Saturday.

Pontypridd (Bus Stn) – A470 – Nelson – Treharris – Merthyr Vale – Troedyrhiw – Merthyr Tydfil (Bus Stn). Hourly Monday–Saturday with extra journeys between Treharris and Merthyr Tydfil: *generally two-hourly Sunday after 2 p.m, with Sunday journeys operating also via Cilfynydd and Aberfan.*

Bedlinog – Nelson – Treharris – Aberfan – Troedyrhiw – Merthyr Tydfil (Bus Stn). Hourly Monday–Saturday; *Two-hourly Sunday after 2 p.m.*

Merthyr Tydfil (Bus Stn) – Cefn Coed – Trefechan – Pontsticill. Generally two-hourly Monday–Saturday. *Generally two-hourly Sunday after 2 p.m.*

Stagecoach Red and White, Telephone enquiry service 01633 266336. Note, many services are subject to change after September 1998. You are advised to check with the enquiry line if you intend to travel after this date.

40   Hereford (Rail Stn)* – Hay-on-Wye – Brecon – Hay-on-Wye – Hereford (Stn). Two per day, Monday to Saturday. *Connects with trains to/from Crewe & Shrewsbury. *Beacon Bus pilot Sunday service to operate 9 sundays plus August Bank Holiday, Summer 1998.*

21   Cardiff* – Newport* – Abergavenny* (Rail Stn) – Abergavenny Town – Crickhowell – Talybont-on-Usk – Brecon – Libanus Mountain Centre – Brecon – Talybont-on-Usk – Crickhowell – Abergavenny Town – Abergavenny* – (Rail Stn) Newport* Cardiff*. *Denotes rail link, two per day, Monday to Saturday plus one service starting from and terminating in Abergavenny.

43   Cardiff – Pontypridd – Merthyr Tydfil – Storey Arms – Libanus – Brecon – Libanus – Storey Arms – Merthyr Tyfil – Pontypridd – Cardiff. Two per day.

63/126   Swansea – Dan yr Ogof – Sennybridge – Brecon – Sennybridge – Dan yr Ogof – Swansea. Two per day.

X4   Cardiff (Bus Stn) – A470 – Pontypridd (Bus Stn) – A470 – Merthyr Tydfil (Bus Stn) – Tredegar – Abergavenny. Hourly Monday–Saturday.

20   Abercanaid – Merthyr Tydfil (Bus Stn). Hourly Monday–Saturday.

24–26   Merthyr Tydfil (Bus Stn) – Cefn Coed – Trefechan – Pontsticill. Every fifteen minutes Monday–Saturday to Trefechan, but only two-hourly Monday–Saturday to Pontsticill.

X38   Cardiff (Bus Stn) – A470 – Pontypridd (Bus Stn) – A470 – Fiddlers Elbow – Nelson – Bargoed. Hourly Monday–Saturday.

78–81   Nelson – Treharris – Edwardsville – Merthyr Vale – Aberfan – Troedyrhiw – Merthyr Tydfil (Bus Stn). Hourly Monday–Saturday from Nelson but usually three per hour from Treharris and more frequent from Aberfan where some journeys serve Bryngolau at the southern end of the village.

X78   Cardiff (Bus Stn) – A470 – Pontypridd (Bus Stn) – A470 – Fiddlers Elbow – Treharris – Edwardsville – Merthyr Vale – Troedyrhiw – Merthyr Tydfil (Bus Stn). Hourly Monday–Saturday but most journeys only operate between Pontypridd and Merthyr Tydfil.

X40   Cardiff (Bus Stn) – A470 – Treforest (Ind Est) – A470 – Merthyr Tydfil (Bus Stn) – Tredegar – Brynmawr. One journey in each direction per day.

21   Newport – Cwmbran – Pontypool – Abergavenny – Talybont-on-Usk – Brecon. Approximately two-hourly Monday–Saturday. *Pilot Sundat service to operate during summer 1998*

39   Brecon (Square) – Talgarth – Hay-on-Wye – Peterchurch – Hereford – Peterchurch – Hay-on-Wye – Talgarth – Brecon. Approximately two hourly Monday to Saturday. *Pilot Sunday service to operate during the Summer 1998.*

X75   Merthyr Tydfil (Bus Stn) – Twyncarmel – Hirwaun – Glynneath – Aberdulais – Swansea (Quadrant Bus Stn). Hourly Monday–Saturday.

B. Accommodation and General Information

Tourist Information Centres

All of the following offer an accommodation booking service, but this is available to personal callers only and a deposit may be required. However, the TICs also keep local accommodation lists and can issue the telephone numbers of local hotels, guest-houses, etc. over the phone.

Brecon	Market Car Park, Brecon, Powys, LD3 9DA. Telephone Brecon (01874) 622485. Open all year.
Cardiff	8–14 Bridge Street, Cardiff, CF5 2EJ. Telephone Cardiff (01222) 227281. Open all year.
Caerphilly	Old Police Station, Park Lane, Caerphilly, CF8 1AA. Telephone Caerphilly (01222) 851378. Seasonal opening.
Merthyr Tydfil	14a Glebeland Street, Merthyr Tydfil, CF47 8AU. Telephone Merthyr (01685) 379884. Open all year.
Pontypridd	The Historical and Cultural Centre, The Old Bridge, Pontypridd, CF37 3PE. Telephone Pontypridd (01443) 402077. Open all year.

Youth Hostels

There are youth hostels at Ty'n-y-Caeau (near Brecon), Llwyn-y-Celyn (near Storey Arms) and Roath Park, Cardiff. For further details, contact the Youth Hostels Association, Trevelyan House, 8 St Stephen's Hill, St Albans, Herts., AL1 2DY. Telephone St Albans (01727) 855215.

Weather Forecasts

The Met. Office provides a 24-hour service of recorded weather information and forecasts via its 'Weathercall' numbers.

Glamorgan	0891 500409
Powys	0891 500414

General

Brecon Beacons National Park Information Centre, Market Car Park, Brecon, Powys, LD3 9AD. Telephone Brecon (01874) 623156.

Brecon Beacons National Park, 7 Glamorgan Street, Brecon, Powys, LD3 7DP. Telephone Brecon (01874) 624437.

Brecon Beacons Mountain Centre, Libanus, Brecon, Powys, LD3 8ER. Telephone Brecon (01874) 623366.

Wales Tourist Board, Brunel House, 2 Fitzalan Road, Cardiff, South Glamorgan, CF2 1UY. Telephone Cardiff (01222) 499909.

C. Useful Addresses

Backpackers Club, PO Box 381, Reading, Berks., RG4 5YY. Telephone Reading (01491) 680684.

British Trust for Conservation Volunteers, Wales Regional Office, Forest Farm, Forest Farm Road, Cardiff, CF4 7JH. Telephone Cardiff (01222) 520990.

British Waterways, Willow Grange, Church Road, Watford, Herts., WD1 3QA. Telephone Watford (01923) 226422.

British Waterways, South Wales Regional Office, The Wharf, Govilon, Abergavenny, Gwent, NP7 9NY. Telephone Gilwern (01873) 830328.

Campaign for the Protection of Rural Wales (Ymgyrch Diogelu Cymru Wledig), Ty Gwyn, 31 High Street, Welshpool, Powys, SY21 7JP. Telephone Welshpool (01938) 552525/556212.

Cardiff Cycling Campaign, Membership Secretary, 33 The Balcony, Castle Arcade, Cardiff CF1 2BY.

Countryside Council for Wales, Plas Penrhos, Ffordd Penrhos, Bangor, LL57 2LQ. Telephone Bangor (01248) 370444.

Cyclists Touring Club, 69 Meadrow, Godalming, Surrey, GU7 3HS. Telephone Godalming (01483) 417217.

Environment Wales, Prince of Wales Committee, 4th Floor, Empire House, Mount Stuart Square, Cardiff, CF1 6DN. Telephone Cardiff (01222) 471121.

Friends of the Earth Cymru, 33 The Balcony, Castle Arcade, Cardiff, CF1 2BY. Telephone Cardiff (01222) 229577.

Inland Waterways Association, 114 Regents Park Road, London, NW1 8UQ. Telephone 0171 586 2510/2556.

Merthyr & Cynon Groundwork Trust, Fedw Hir, Llwydcoed, Aberdare, CF44 0DX. Telephone Aberdare (01685) 883880.

Offa's Dyke Association, Offa's Dyke Centre, West Street, Knighton, Powys, LD7 1EW. Telephone Knighton (01547) 528753.

Ordnance Survey, Romsey Road, Maybush, Southampton, Hants., SO9 4DH. Telephone Southampton (01703) 792000.

Railway Ramblers, 47a Stondon Park, Forest Hill, London, SE23 1LB.

Ramblers Association, 1–5 Wandsworth Road, London, SW8 2XX. Telephone 0171 582 6878.

Royal Commission on Ancient and Historical Monuments in Wales, Edelston House, Queen's Road, Aberystwyth, Dyfed, SY23 2HP. Telephone Aberystwyth (01970) 621233.

Sustrans Ltd, 35 King Street, Bristol, Avon, BS1 4DZ. Telephone Bristol (0117) 9268893.

Taff Trail Project, c/o Merthyr & Cynon Groundwork Trust (address as above).

Wales Tourist Board (Bwrdd Croeso Cymru), Brunel House, 2 Fitzalan Road, Cardiff, CF2 1UY. Telephone Cardiff (01222) 499909.

Youth Hostels Association, Trevelyan House, 8 St Stephen's Hill, St Albans, Herts., AL1 2DY. Telephone St Albans (01727) 855215.

D. Other Long-Distance Trails in Wales

Most of the existing long-distance recreational routes in Wales are for walkers, with cyclists poorly catered for on off-road routes if at all. However, in an attempt to redress this, a number of local authorities are working on projects similar to the Taff Trail, although they could all do with a catalyst to speed up their implementation. Long-distance cycling routes currently being considered or constructed include the following:

1. Brecon to Newport
2. Cardiff to Newport
3. Cardiff to Swansea
4. Swansea to Hay-on-Wye

In most cases, these projects are hampered both by shortage of funds and lack of central coordination. There is plenty of scope here for Groundwork or other organizations to get involved and help out.

The most significant local cycling facilities are to be found in Swansea, where the Swansea Bikepath Network is 14 miles long and growing, and at Afan Argoed Country Park (on the A4107 north-east of Port Talbot), where there is a 15 mile network of interconnecting routes built almost entirely on disused railways. Both of these will eventually be integrated into the long-distance schemes listed above.

For walkers, there is already a wide choice of routes, the principal long-distance paths being listed below:

1. The Coed Morgannwg Way (36 miles). Runs from Gethin Woodland Park near Merthyr Tydfil and on the Taff Trail, to Margam Country Park, near Port Talbot. Further details from Afan Argoed Country Park, Cynonville, Port Talbot, West Glamorgan, SA13 3HG. Telephone Cymmer (01639) 850564.

2. The Ffordd y Bryniau Ridgeway Walk (21 miles). Runs from Mynydd y Gaer to Caerphilly Common and crosses the Taff Trail just south of Nantgarw. Further details from Leisure Services Department, Taff Ely Borough Council, 37 Mill Street, Pontypridd, Mid Glamorgan, CF37 2TU. Telephone Pontypridd (01443) 485888.

3. The Ogwr Ridgeway Walk (13 miles). Runs from Margam Country Park to Mynydd y Gaer north of Pencoed, where it connects with the Ffordd y Bryniau Ridgeway Walk. Further details from Borough Planning Officer, Ogwr Borough Council, Civic Offices, Angel Street, Bridgend, Mid Glamorgan, CF31 1LX. Telephone Bridgend (01656) 643643.

4. The Rhymney Valley Ridgeway Walk (27 miles). A circular route along the three ridges of Mynydd y Grug, Thornhill and Eglwysilan which takes in Machen, Hengoed and Caerphilly. Further details from Caerphilly Mountain Countryside Service, The Taff Gorge Countryside Centre, Heol y Fforest, Tongwynlais, Cardiff, CF4 7JR. Telephone Caerphilly (01222) 813356.

5. Glyndwr's Way (120 miles). A circular route in mid-Wales linking Knighton, Welshpool, Llanwddyn, Machynlleth and Llanidloes. Further details from Powys County Council, County Hall, Llandrindod Wells, Powys, LD1 5LG. Telephone Llandrindod Wells (01597) 826000.

6. Offa's Dyke Path (168 miles). A long-distance path along the Welsh border from Chepstow to Prestatyn. Further details from Offa's Dyke Association, Old Primary School, West Street, Knighton, Powys, LD7 1EW. Telephone Knighton (01547) 528753.

7. The Pembrokeshire Coast Path (168 miles). A long-distance path along the dramatic Pembrokeshire coast from Cardigan to Amroth. Further details from Pembrokeshire Coast National Park, County Offices, Haverfordwest, Dyfed, SA61 1QZ. Telephone Haverfordwest (01437) 4591. See also Brian John, *The Pembrokeshire Coast Path*, Countryside Commission and others, 1989.

GLOSSARY

This glossary is based on the text of the present volume. It contains a few names for which one has preferred not to offer a speculative explanation. Where explanation is possible limited space has required it be given in great brevity. These notes owe much to the research of the late Ifor Williams, Melville Richards, and R.J. Thomas. The following abbreviations are used: **W** (Welsh); **L** (Latin); **E** (English); **Ir.** (Irish); **pn** (personal name).

ABERCANAID: More correctly, ABERCANNAID: the confluence of the Cannaid (bright/gleaming) river and the River Taf.

ABERCYNON: Confluence of the River Cynon (with the Taf).

ABERDARE: Derived of the local **W** pronunciation of ABERDAR: confluence of the River Dar with the River Cynon.

ABERFAN: Confluence of the Rivers Fan and Taf. 'Fan' probably derives from the name of the mountain between the Merthyr and Cynon Valleys (ban/fan = peak/crest).

ABERGAVENNY: The confluence of the Gefenni/Gafenni/Fenni river with the Usk. *Gobannium* is related to the **W** plural noun 'gofain(t)' (blacksmiths) and to the **pn** of that mythical character in the Mabinogion named Gofannon.

AFON CAERFANELL: Afon = river. 'Crafnell' is related to the **W** verb 'crafu' (to scrape/rake/scratch) and the **Ir.** *crobh* (paw/ claw/hand from wrist to fingers). The suffix '-ell' is a diminutive. Thus the name describes the eroding action of the river.

AFON CYNRIG: Afon = river; Cynrig = an old **pn** (Cynfrig/Cynwrig/Cynrig).

AFON MENASCIN: The original **W** forms are MANHASGIN/MENHASGIN. 'Ma-' (meadow/plain) and possibly an **Ir.** derived **pn**, 'Hesgyn'. Also possible is the **W** compound 'hesgin' (hesg + in): 'where sedge grows'.

AFON TARELL: Afon = river. The second element was originally either TRYDARELL or TARDDERELL. The former, the raucous sound of the river (trydar); the latter, its gushing course (tarddu).

BARGOED: Originally BARGOD (feminine noun: Y Fargod). Found in many placenames, especially with rivers: edge/limit/ border/side.

BARRY: Customarily in **W** Y BARRI. Probably derived of the archaic **W** noun 'barren/bar' (hill) abbreviated barren/ barre/barri to give Y Barri (The Hill).

BASSALEG: Properly in **W** BASALEG. Derived from the **L** 'basilica': church.

BLAENGLYN: Head (blaen) of the valley (glyn).

BRECON: The **E** forms BRECON/BRECKNOCK, both ultimately derived of the **W** BRYCHEINIOG based on **pn** BRYCHAN. Name of a semi-mythical figure of **Ir.** extraction who ruled the district in the mid-5th century AD. The **W** name of Brecon town is ABERHONDDU: confluence (aber) of the pleasant river (hawdd + ni) and the Usk (Wysg).

BRYNICH: Probably based on the **Ir.** derived **pn** Brynych, one of the sons of the local ruler Brychan Brycheiniog.

BRYN OER: Cold (oer) hill.

CAERLEON: Its full form in **W** is CAERLLION-AR-WYSG: the fortress of the legions on the Usk.

CAERPHILLY: From the **W** CAERFFILI. The 'caer' element is simple: fortress. The second element may be derived of a **pn**.

CANTREF: Early **W** territorial unit twice the extent of a 'cwmwd' generally containing a hundred homesteads (cant + tref).

CARDIFF: In **W** CAERDYDD. Both forms are derived of the original **W** CAERDYF: 'fortress on the Taf'.

CASTELL COCH: Red Castle.

CEFN COED Y CYMER: 'Cefn' denotes a ridge: thus, CEFN COED would signify a wooded ridge. The final element, CYMER, refers to the confluence of the Taf Fawr and Taf Fechan rivers.

CEFN CRUG: Hump (crug) ridge.

CEFN GLAS: Green ridge. In earlier **W** the Celtic-derived 'glas' denoted the colours green and grey as well as blue.

CILFYNYDD: Mountain (mynydd) recess (cil).

COED CAEDYRYS: Wood (coed) of the difficult/hard (dyrys) field (cae).

COEDPENMAEN: Properly, COED PEN MAEN: wood at/of the top of the stone (maen).

CRAIG CERRIG GLEISIAD: First element a large rock or rocky outcrop, the second 'stones'. Third element suggests the colours blue/grey.

CRICKHOWEL: Properly, CRUG-HYWEL – from whence 'Crucywel' also: Hywel's knoll.

CYFARTHFA: Its elements are CYFARTH (to bark/barking) + -FA (place); its precise origins unknown.

CYNON: Possibly a **pn** or possibly descriptive of the river concerned being swift and noisome.

DARREN FAWR: Great rocky ridge (tarren).

DOL-Y-GAER: Castle meadow.

DOWLAIS: A compound of DU + GLAIS: black/dark river/stream – the opposite of 'gwynlais' as in Tongwynlais (below).

DYNEA: Tentatively related to the archaic **W** noun 'dynn' (as in tyddyn/treuddyn/llystyn), indicating the location of one or more buildings.

DYNEVOR: Properly, DINEFWR. 'Din-' signifies a fortress or stronghold. An archaic noun 'efwr' which means shelter/ hedge; the same word also exists to indicate 'cow-parsley'.

EGLWYSILAN: Church of Ilan, shadowy 6th-century Christian. Its previous name was Merthyr Ilan (*see* Merthyr Tudful below).

FENNI FACH: FENNI related to Gafenni in Abergavenny (above). FACH: little/small.

FFOREST FAWR: Great forest/wood.

FFRWDGRECH: Loud/vehement (croch) stream/torrent (ffrwd).

FFRWD UCHAF: Upper (uchaf) stream/torrent (ffrwd).

GABALFA: Corruption of (Y) GEUBALFA: a place (-fa) where a boat (ceubal) ferried one across the River Taf.

GARWNANT: Rough/turbulent (garw) stream (nant).

GETHIN: Originally CETHIN: dark/dusky/dun; subsequently a **pn** thereafter surname.

GILWERN: Properly, Y GILWERN. 'Cil' (recess/nook/rear) and 'gwern' (a site where alders grow; also 'swamp').

GLANRHYD: Side/shore/bank (glan) of the ford (rhyd).

GLYNDYRUS: Properly, GLYNDYRYS: difficult/hard (dyrys) valley.

GLYNTAFF: Accurately, GLYN-TAF: Taf valley.

GOVILON: Current **W** form GOFILON needs further investigation.

GRON-FELEN: The components appear to be 'cron' (round) and 'felen' (yellow); but on their own they are insufficient to explain.

GURNOS: A farm name: properly Y GURNOS. The most plausible view is that 'y gurnos' is a diminutive of the feminine singular noun 'cyrn/curn' meaning peak/mound/ pile/stack. Thus, 'Y Gurnos': 'the little hill'.

HENGOED: Old wood.

LLANDAFF: Properly, LLANDAF: Church beside the Taf.

LLANFAES: Now a 'suburb' of Brecon town, but originally a distinct settlement on the other side of the Usk: llan (church); maes/faes (open field).

LLANFOIST: The **W** original LLANFFWYST. While 'llan' (church) is simple, the second element must be considered further.

LLANFRYNACH: The church of Brynach (**pn**).

LLANGATTOCK: An anglicization of LLANGADOG much aided by the dialect pronunciation 'Llan-gatog/c': the church of the fifth-century Christian leader of royal background, Cadog.

LLANGYNIDR: The church of Cynidr (**pn**).

LLANOFER: The church (llan) of St Myfor or Mofor.

LLWYN-ONN: Ash (onn) grove (llwyn).

LLWYN-Y-CELYN: Holly (celyn) bush/grove.

LLWYNYREOS: Nightingale (eos) grove (llwyn). Best written LLWYN-YR-EOS.

MACHEN: MA- (meadow/plain) + CAIN (probably a feminine **pn**). Brychan Brycheiniog had a daughter of this name. The final element may relate to the adjective 'cain' (fair/beautiful).

MELINGRIFFITH: More correctly, MELIN-GRUFFYDD: Gruffydd's Mill.

MERTHYR TYDFIL: A name denoting the 'martyrium' (**L**: shrine/burial place) of the (female) saint Tudful.

MORLAIS: The elements are 'mawr' (great) and 'glais' (river/stream).

MYNYDD MEIO: Mynydd: mountain. MEIO may be a fond form of the old masculine **pn** Mai or of the archaic feminine noun 'mai' (field): plural 'meiau'.

NANT CWM LLWCH: The first and second elements are simply 'stream' and 'valley'. The third is not the noun 'llwch' meaning 'dust', but the archaic noun 'llwch' a lake/bog/- marsh/saturated ground/ standing water.

NANT DDU: Black/dark brook.

NANTGARW: The original form Nant-y-Carw (Coch): Stag Stream, subsequently shortened and mutated to NANT-GARW.

NEATH: From the **W** NEDD, derived of the Brythonic root 'Nida'. This river name was adopted by the Romans to identify their fort built alongside its waters: hence 'Nidum'. Its exact meaning is uncertain.

NEUADD: Literally, 'hall'; alternately 'great house'. Originally a farm, now a reservoir.

PENARTH: PEN-ARTH: top/crest of the hill.

PENCELLI: Top/end of the grove (celli).

PENMAILLARD: Most probably a corruption of Pen-moel-allt (see below), to which it is adjacent in the upper Taf Valley.

PENMOELALLT: Pen-moel-allt: top/crest of the bare hill.

PENRHOS: Top/crest of the moor.

PENTIR RHIW: Hill(y) headland.

PENTWYN: Top/crest of the hill (twyn).

PENTWYN-ISAF: Pen-twyn = hill top/crest. Isaf (lower/lowest), usually denotes agricultural property bearing same name as other properties in the vicinity: for example uchaf (upper) or canol (middle).

PENTYRCH: Boar's head: PEN + TWRCH (twrch>tyrch).

PEN-Y-DARREN: Top/summit of the rocky ridge (tarren).

PEN-Y-GROES: Head, or end, of the cross (croes): sometimes referring to an actual cross; more often signifying crossroads.

PEN-Y-LAN: Top (pen) of the hillside (glan).

PONTCANNA: Bridge of Canna: final element held to be a **pn**, possibly an early Christian figure (*cp*. Llan-gan in the Vale of Glamorgan).

PONT MAES MAWR: Great-field bridge.

PONTSARN: Pont = bridge; sarn = road/way; also 'stepping stones'.

PONTSTICILL: Pont-sticill: bridge (at/of the) stile.

PONT-Y-DDERWEN: Oak bridge.

PONT-Y-GWAITH: Bridge of works (usually early ironworks).

PONTYMOILE: In full, LLANFIHANGEL PONT-Y-MOEL, a village in the parish of Pant-teg, Gwent: the church of St Michael (at) the bare hill bridge.

PONTYPOOL: A hybrid of **W** pont (bridge) and **E** 'pool'.

PONTYPRIDD: Originally 'PONTY-Y-TY-PRIDD': 'bridge at the earthen house' – a reference to a primitive cottage which stood at one end of the famous single-arched stone bridge built by William Edwards in 1756.

RADYR: More properly RADUR: derived of 'Yr Oradur' (**L** 'oratorium') signifying church/chapel/prayer-house.

RHONDDA: Properly in **W** Y RHONDDA. Originally Rhoddne/Rhoddna probably based on element 'rhawdd' (as in *adrawdd/ adrodd*: to recite) + suffix '-ne' (river/stream): thus raucous/noisome river.

RHYD-Y-CAR: Cart ford: where farmers of pre-industrial Merthyr Tudful crossed the River Taf in wagons.

RHYDYFELIN: Properly RHYD-FELEN: yellow ford.

RHYMNEY/RUMNEY: Properly, RHYMNI. The initial element 'rhwmp': an old term for a gimlet, auger or borer – carpenter's tool for cutting a hole in wood. The second element, '-ni' is a common suffix denoting a river. The name therefore describes the river boring or gouging into the ground over which it flows.

ROATH: From the **W** Y RHATH, itself derived of **Ir**. *rath*: fort/stronghold.

SENGHENNYDD: The name of a medieval administrative unit chiefly between the Rivers Taf and Rhymni. Element '-ydd' signifies territory, remainder is derived of the plausible but unattested **pn** 'Sangan'.

TAFF: Properly TAF (**W** 'f' = **E** 'v'). Ancient river name of possibly pre-Celtic origin. Preferred theories are 'dark water' or merely 'water'.

TAF FECHAN: Little, or Lesser, Taf (see above).

TALYBONT-ON-USK: 'Tal' in a placename indicates the 'far end' of feature, e.g. bridge (Tal-y-bont). River name 'Usk' is derived of the **W** original WYSG. This is held by many to be related to the Old **Ir**. noun *esc* (water); but on a number of grounds this was rejected by Sir Ifor Williams, who related the river name to *eisc* (fish).

TAL-Y-LLYN: End/top/head of the lake (llyn): see Tal-y-bont above.

TONGWYNLAIS: TON-GWYN-LAIS: sward/meadow of the clear/bright stream.

TORPANTAU: Tor-pantau: breach (in the) valleys.

TRALLWNG/TRALLWN: TRALLWM is another variant. The elements are TRA- (exceedingly) and LLWNG/LLWNC (permeable). Thus, land named 'trallwng' would be very sodden or boggy.

TREDEGAR: The initial part is TRE(F): farm/home. The next word is an old **pn** TEGYR mutated and varied to give '-degar'.

TREFECHAN: Small settlement/town.

TREFFOREST: Modern **W** 'tre/tref' = a town. Its primary meaning was farm/home/homestead; 'fforest' is self-evident.

TREFIL: Tre(f) = farm/home/homestead. The second element needs further consideration.

TROED-Y-RHIW: Foot (troed) of the hill (rhiw).

TWM BRIDGE: **W** form of the **pn** 'Tom', or corruption of 'twyn' (hill).

TY RHIW: Hill house.

VAYNOR: Anglicization of (Y) FAENOR. Name said originally to have been Maenor Wynno: after the 6th-century Christian pioneer Gwynno to whom the local church is dedicated. While 'maenor/maenol' subsequently acquired lordly association by proximity to **E** 'manor', the term/s originally denoted a unit of territory in **W** law: tyddyn/rhandir/gafael/tref/ maenol.

YNYSANGHARAD: The river-meadow (ynys) of Angharad (**pn**).

YNYSFACH: Small river-meadow (ynys).

Glossary compiled by D.L. Davies.

BIBLIOGRAPHY

General and Historical

Barrie, D.S.M., *A Regional History of the Railways of Great Britain, Volume 12: South Wales*, David and Charles, 1980.
——, *The Barry Railway*, Oakwood Press, 1962.
——, *The Brecon and Merthyr Railway*, Oakwood Press, 1980 (4th impression).
Hadfield, Charles, *British Canals, An Illustrated History*, David and Charles, 1984 (7th edition).
——, *Canals of South Wales and the Border*, David and Charles, 1967 (2nd edition).
Morgan, H., *South Wales Branch Lines*, Ian Allan, 1984.
Page, James, *Forgotten Railways, Volume 8: South Wales*, David and Charles, 1988 (2nd edition).
Russell, Ronald, *Lost Canals of England and Wales*, David and Charles, 1971.
Various, *Brecon Beacons and Mid Wales*, AA/Ordnance Survey, 1989.

Literature on the Taff Trail

Gillham, Mary, Perkins, John and Thomas, Clive, *The Historic Taff Valley: Quakers Yard to Aberfan*, D. Brown & Sons Ltd, 1979.
Hodgson, Malcolm, *The Taff Trail for Walkers and Cyclists: A Provisional Route Linking Cardiff and Brecon*, Taff Trail Project, 1992. Provides sectional sketch maps of the whole route from Brecon to Cardiff.
Hodgson, M., Littlewood, K., Williams, A.A., *From the Valley to the Bay: A Scenic Walk from Merthyr Tydfil to Cardiff*, Taff Trail Project, 1991. A 22 mile walk from Merthyr to Cardiff, following parts of the Taff Trail and various alternative routes.
Littlewood, Kevin, *Taff Trails: Short Walks in the Taff Valley*, Taff Trail Project, 1990. A series of linear and circular walks in the Taff Valley, some of them following parts of the Taff Trail.
——, *The Taff Trail Inventory, 1990–91*, Taff Trail Project, 1991.
——, *The Taff Trail: Merthyr to Brecon Circular Walk*, Taff Trail Project, 1990. Describes the westerly and easterly routes from Merthyr to Brecon.
——, *Vaynor Circular Walks*, Taff Trail Project, 1990. A series of circular walks based on the Taff Trail around Cefn Coed and Pontsarn.
Merthyr Tydfil and District Naturalists' Society, *The Historic Taff Valley: Brecon Beacons National Park*, D. Brown & Sons Ltd, 1982.
——, *The Historic Taff Valley: Merthyr Tydfil to Aberfan*, D. Brown & Sons Ltd, 1984.

The Taff Trail is also promoted by an extensive series of leaflets, copies of which may be obtained from local Tourist Information Centres.

INDEX

QUESTIONNAIRE

Please take a few moments to complete this questionnaire and return it to:

Merthyr and Cynon Groundwork Trust
Fedw Hir
Llwydcoed
ABERDARE
Mid Glamorgan
CF44 0DX

GENERAL QUESTIONS – PLEASE TICK ONE ONLY PER QUESTION

1. **How did you find out about the Taff Trail?**

   Always known about it ☐   Word of mouth ☐

   Magazines/Newspapers ☐   Leaflets ☐

   Discovered by Accident ☐   TV/Radio ☐

   Guidebook ☐   Others,
   Please specify ....

2. **Where did you buy the book?**

   Bookshop ☐   Youth Hostel ☐

   Sports shop ☐   Museum ☐

   Tourist Information ☐   Groundwork Trust ☐
   Centre

   Others,
   Please specify ....

3. **Did you buy the book for?**

   Exploring the entire length of the Trail ☐

   Exploring sections of the Trail ☐

   Reading only ☐

   Research ☐

   Others, please specify ....

4. **How would you rate the following in the book?**

	GOOD	SATISFACTORY	POOR
Directions			
Maps			
Photographs			
Text			
Cover			
Value for money			

USE OF THE TAFF TRAIL

1. **What is the purpose of your use of the Trail?**

   Walking for pleasure ☐   Cycling for pleasure ☐

   Jogging for pleasure ☐   Walking the dog ☐

   Walking to/from   Cycling to/from
   school/work/ shop/   school/work/shop/
   family/pub etc ....   family/pub etc ....

2. **How often do you use the Trail?**

   More than once a week ☐   Once a week ☐

   Monthly ☐   Less than monthly ☐

   First visit ☐

3. **How would you rate the following items?**

	GOOD	SATISFACTORY	POOR	NO COMMENT
Surfacing				
Condition of benches/picnic sites				
Signposting				
Usefulness of leaflets/ booklets/other				

4. **How would you rate the control of the following on the Trail?**

	GOOD	SATISFACTORY	POOR	NO COMMENT
Litter				
Dog mess				
Vandalism/ graffiti				

5. **Have you any comments you would like to make on the Taff Trail or the Guidebook?**

   Thank you for your time and comments. The Taff Trail Project strives to improve your enjoyment of the countryside.